ILL MET
BY GASLIGHT

By the same author

Novels
Change and Decay in all around I see
The Last Peacock

Criticism
Muriel Spark

ILL MET
BY GASLIGHT

Five Edinburgh Murders

Allan Massie

Paul Harris Publishing

Edinburgh

© Allan Massie 1980

First published 1980 by
PAUL HARRIS PUBLISHING
25 London Street
Edinburgh

ISBN 0 904505 92 8

Photoset printed and bound in Great Britain by
REDWOOD BURN LIMITED
Trowbridge and Esher

For Euan Cameron

in affection and with gratitude.

Contents

Introduction

Murder may be taken as the breaking-point of civil society. It is that moment when bonds of interest and affection, which commonly act as a restraint on the passions and the individual will, are severed; the murderer rejects the authority of society, and, in doing so, proclaims himself an alien. In society we live amicably by accepting limitations placed on our freedom to exercise our will. We commonly accept those limitations willingly, recognising, if only tacitly or unconsciously, that they are the obverse of society's duty to protect our own Persons and Property. As Burke put it in his *Reflections on the Revolution in France*, 'Man cannot enjoy the rights of an uncivil and of a civil state together. That he may obtain justice he gives up his right of determining what it is in points the most essential to him. That he may secure some liberty, he makes a surrender in trust of the whole of it.' It is this convention, on which civil society is properly based, that the murderer rejects, asserting instead his own right 'to be his own Governor'. For this reason, because the act of murder threatens to tear apart the whole social fabric, society has always recoiled in aversion from the murderer. Common humanity is revolted by this act; he, setting himself above the law, is set by us without it. Murder therefore takes place at a crossroads where the will of the individual diverges from the code society has imposed.

It is easy to romanticise the murderer. That attitude is implicit in the greatest novel to centre on murder, Dostoevsky's *Crime and Punishment*; even though Dostoevsky himself does not fall into the trap, his careless readers may. Inasmuch as society is felt to be oppressive, to impose restrictive, diminishing conventions, then the Free Man, a rebel against its dominion, may be fascinated by the act of murder. You can see that in the existential attraction to the *acte gratuit*, the motiveless murder, the one that exists simply as a gob of spittle in society's face. Such identification with the murderer is dangerous; he acts out the unconscious fantasies of others. Looked at this way, public obsession with the most hideous crimes takes on a new ugliness; the cries of outrage too easily resembling the rage of the mirrored Caliban; the beast in all of us shrieking for release. Of course, at the same time, we enjoy the equally deep, and wholly conscious, pleasure of reprobation, the experience of our own moral superiority and the reassurance that we at least are comfortably settled in society.

Seen in this way, the murderer has a heavy symbolic load to bear. Seen more closely he is rarely up to the job. For, of course, it is only in Fiction and sometimes in his own imagination that the murderer approaches the Nietzschean Superman. In that cold reality that so often ends in a grey dawn he is too often quite the reverse; not someone who transcends the social norm, but rather one incapable of measuring up to it; *untermensch* not *übermensch*. When one sees the public rage poured on these miserable incompetents one sees society at its most unpleasant. For, while the murderer represents the failure of social man, society can hardly altogether escape some responsibility. To say that is not to slide into the imbecilities enshrined in the cant phrase, 'we are all guilty'; merely to say that for society callously to cast out social failures may accord with some Darwinian theories of how to behave, but is hardly civilised or humane.

Because murder happens at that point when the demands of the individual Will, the Ego, clash with the duties ordained by society, a study of murders and murderers may help to illuminate our nature in both its social and its secret aspects. Different epochs give rise to different sorts of murder. The *crime passionel*, for instance, was long rare in Anglo-Saxon countries, common in Latin ones, not because Latins were more passionate, or more violent than Englishmen, but because their social conception of what became a man decreed that in certain circumstances he should slay his mistress or his wife, or the woman's lover. That may seem to contradict what has been said about the clash between individual and society which murder represents; it does not really do so however; these were murderers, on the point of social acceptibility, still of course illegal, but in that particular society more easily understood, more easily forgiven. For attitudes to murder change according to social developments; some kinds are always more reprehensible than others. For this reason a study of murders offers valuable lessons in sociology.

For a long time domestic murders were peculiarly British; they are no longer so common. The reasons are doubtless various, but essentially domestic murder was the result of the elevation of the family to a position of extreme importance, while at the same time the cult of respectability was practised and divorce was difficult and disgraceful. Such a combination set up conflicts in the individual which were too often resolved in murder, as the cases of Bennison and Chantrelle described here illustrate. In our lifetime all these – family, respectability, sanctity of marriage – have been relaxed. It is no longer necessary to murder to gratify your lust, or please the Ego; hence, domestic murders are rarer. Yet at the same time the naked commercialism of our society, allied to vaguely articulated but widely diffused notions of self-realisation, has spawned all sorts of sexual fantasy; this may be seen as a social tendency, but sociey does not move as fast as the individual imagination; things are still illegal; murders take place in consequence. (I am not of course advocating still further liberation in this respect; merely indicating how social tendencies, worked up by the fantasising individual imagination, will frequently have anti-social results.)

Recognition of how forms of murder respond to social developments should make us wary of theories concerning criminal types. First, murder is in some ways an unusual criminal action, a good many murderers leading otherwise law-abiding lives. Too much should not be made of this difference however; essentially murder is like all other crimes in its rejection of the obligations which society tries to impose on the individual. However, the second point is more important. A man, law-abiding in certain circumstances, becomes criminal in others; that is to say, the same man may find one

3

INTRODUCTION

society acceptable in its demands, another not. You can see this difference manifested by problem children, who suddenly, removed to a new school or a new environment, become reformed. The essential self has not changed; but has merely found society against which it is not necessary to rebel. Talk of criminal types is always glib:

> 'In a popular magazine there is one of the usual articles about criminology; about whether wicked men could be made good if their heads were taken to pieces. As by far the wickedest men I know of are much too rich and powerful ever to submit to the process, the speculation leaves me cold. I always notice with pain, however, a curious absence of the portraits of living millionaires from such galleries of awful examples; most of the portraits in which we are called upon to remark the line of the nose or the curve of the forehead appear to be the portraits of ordinary sad men, who stole because they were hungry or killed because they were in a rage. The physical peculiarity seems to vary infinitely; sometimes it is the remarkable square head, sometimes it is the unmistakable round head; sometimes the learned draw attention to the abnormal development, sometimes to the striking deficiency, of the back of the head. I have tried to discover what is the invariable factor, the one permanent mark of the scientific criminal type; after exhaustive classification I have to come to the conclusion that it consists in being poor.'

So Chesterton, and most of what he says is admirable sense. Even his own ironic conclusion, sentimental though it may be pronounced, can be defended. The poor are more likely than the rich to find society thwarting their will; the obstacles placed in the way of their self-gratification being incomparably greater. So, for example, the first of my subjects, the amiable scoundrel, David Haggart, followed a career which could fairly enough be interpreted as an act of defiance directed at his poverty and social position. It is, I think, possible to identify mental habits and qualities characteristic of the criminal – selfishness, indifference to others' well-being or interests whenever these clash with one's own, disregard of consequence – but, as Chesterton points out, these characteristics are frequently shared by the successful. In any case such criminal attributes can generally only be identified after the criminal act.

This book deals with murders in society. It concentrates less perhaps than some readers might wish on the set-piece, the trial for murder, which concludes my murderers' careers, and it is not pretended that these are cases of the kind likely to give rise to much debate. It is probable that the four who were hanged were guilty of the crimes of which they were accused, and that the one who got away was extremely lucky. Interest lies in the circumstances of the crimes rather than in questions of guilt or innocence. Why were these five people brought to this defiance of society and its laws?

It is also a study of Edinburgh where all five murderers lived, where four of the crimes were committed and four of the murderers hanged. The cases extend from the years just after Waterloo to the 1920's. They shed some light on the development of the city, on changing habits of living, thinking and feeling. It is perhaps a remarkable feature of Edinburgh murders that so many were committed by incomers. Of my subjects only David Haggart and Jessie King were natives of the city, while the most famous of those I have chosen not to deal with, Burke and Hare, were of course Irish immigrants. I doubt whether there is much significance in this fact, though it might be claimed that incomers always find it harder to adapt to the norms of any particular society, and are therefore more likely to find themselves behaving as outlaws.

Any student of Edinburgh crime owes much to William Roughead, its most indefatigable chronicler. Roughead (1870–1952), who as a small boy met Chantrelle, and who attended the trials of Jessie King and Donald Merrett, is a figure worthy of close attention himself. A largely nonpractising solicitor, he attended every major trial in the High Court over a period of more than fifty years, and wrote about most of them. I confess to a certain feeling of guilt towards him and his shade; for I have used him freely and used him roughly. Roughead, very much of his period, was fascinated by crime and deviance, and totally unsympathetic towards criminals. He regarded the Law with absolute reverence and no suspicion whatsoever. It was an attitude that spoke of complete social security – criminals belonged to a lower class – of a lack of any real imagination and of a crude, if effective, psychology. He quite rightly saw that criminals were subversive, and concluded that they were therefore wicked. So he displayed a vengeful relish in his treatment of them that a more squeamish, more sceptical, age may find unattractive. He could not see the ugliness of a society where established authority employed the law to keep the inferior classes in order; or that the criminal might be victim as much as rebel. And, worse than that, he had rarely any idea why the crimes were committed. In short the trouble with Roughead was that he was a judge, not a murderer. That may seem an extraordinary thing to say; at a time when society is under strain it may even sound rather silly. Nevertheless I think it is both true and important to recognise this as a limitation in criminologists such as Roughead. It displays something deficient in their knowledge of, and response to, human nature. He knew why judges put on the black cap, and even what they felt like as they did so; but not why the man in the dock had earned it or how he felt when he saw it donned. Given his place in, and view of, society, that was reasonable enough; you can't however write sense from that standpoint today.

Chesterton saw all this more than half a century ago:

'The secret is,' Father Brown said, 'that it was I who killed all those people. . . . I mean that I really did see myself, and my real self, committing the murders. I didn't actually kill the men by material means, but that's not important. Any brick or bit of machinery might have killed them by material means; but that's not the point. I mean that I thought and thought about how a man might come to be like that, until I realized that I really was like that, in everything except actual final consent to the action. . . . What do these men mean, nine times out of ten . . . when they say criminology is a science? They mean getting *outside* a man and studying him as if he were a gigantic insect; in what they would call a dry impartial light, in what I should call a dead and dehumanized light. They mean getting a long way off him, as if he were a distant prehistoric monster; staring at the shape of his "criminal skull" as if it were a sort of eerie growth, like the horn on a rhinoceros's nose. When a scientist talks about a type, he never means himself, but always his neighbour; probably his poorer neighbour – I don't try to get outside the man. I try to get inside the murderer . . . no man's really any good till he knows how bad he is, or might be; till he's realized exactly how much right he has to all this snobbery, and sneering, and talking about "criminals", as if they were apes in a forest ten thousand miles away; till he's got rid of all the dirty self-deception of talking about low types and deficient skulls; till he's squeezed out of his soul the last drop of the oil of the Pharisees; till his only hope is somehow or other to have captured one criminal, and kept him safe and sane under his own hat. . . .'

I wish I could claim to have risen consistently to this high seriousness; irony and complacency keep breaking in to prevent it. Still Chesterton seems to me preferable to Roughead. He feels with the murderer and realises that the murderer's denial of the claims of humanity is all too human. It may be objected, justly enough, that to attack Roughead and his attitude to crime, is superfluous; no more than flogging a dead donkey; that indeed we have gone too far in the other direction; moral relativism is all the mode; criminals are 'understood', their crimes explained away, their victims ignored; that sociologists of our day, far from talking about criminal types, are only too ready to talk away the existence of crime itself. Treating it merely or at most as a manifestation of anti-social feeling, they demoralise it; and, inasmuch as they are themselves frequently hostile to society as it is presently constituted, they sympathise only too completely with the criminal. In polysyllabic jargon they blur issues and render all actions, except those of the civil authority, morally neutral.

Chesterton would have had no time for this sort of talk either; nor do I. Murder is not to be diminished, and civil society has to be defended. It is right to reprobate the murderer whose victim has suffered an unspeakable wrong. Those who talk fulsomely of social deprivation can hardly be trusted if they are blind to the fact of a more vital deprivation. There is such a thing as evil, and it rejects the claims of humanity. The untrammelled ego will prove destructive, while the Good in Man, the highest Good of which he is capable, is creative.

Yet at the same time it is true that the forms, habits and ideologies of civil society contribute at any time to the formation of the characters of those who murder. So, of my subjects, David Haggart was led into a world of professional criminals that seemed to offer, did indeed offer, that bourgeois desideratum, the career open to talents; it promised a way of life that accorded with his notions of style – the criminal fraternity aped the aristocracy in manners and morals; but it was a way of life which made it very likely that one day, in rage, desperation or in liquor, he would strike and kill. William Bennison, his ego fostered by the balm of his Evangelical religion, was taught erroneously to think that all things were permitted to the Redeemed who had been washed in the Blood of the Lamb. Eugene Marie Chantrelle, embittered by failure, slew his wife, who had only remained tied to him because she feared to lose her children and dreaded the obloquy that separation or divorce would bring her. Jessie King, the Stockbridge baby-farmer, was given her opportunity by a code of morality and social behaviour which ensured that one Edinburgh child in fourteen was born illegitimate. Donald Merrett, voracious as the pike he resembled, was an early modernist, a precursor of the affluent society, intent on self-gratification, dull to obligation. Intensely selfish, he alone swam free to continue destroying. . . .

David Haggart

Or the Coneish Cove

From the Castle Rock at Edinburgh you look across the Forth
to Fife. Today the foreground of the view is covered by buildings that stretch, intermingled with parks, gardens and
playing-fields, all the way to the Firth. At the time of Waterloo, however, only the beginnings of Edinburgh's New
Town had been built, and a gazer from the Rock would soon
have overlooked them. The open Lothian countryside
stretched down to Cramond and the sea. It was on the Rock in
that year that the young George Borrow, author of *Lavengro*
and *The Bible in Spain*, came one day on a lad a few years older
than himself, perched on a promontory and gazing into that
watery distance:

> 'A lad of some fifteen years; he is bare-headed, and his red
> uncombed hair stands on end like a hedgehog's bristles; his
> frame is lithy, like that of an antelope, but he has prodigous
> breadth of chest; he wears a military undress, that of the
> regiment, even of a drummer, for it is Wild Davy, whom a
> month before I had seen enlisted on Leith Links to serve
> King George with drum and drumstick as long as his ser-
> vices were required, and who, ere a week had elapsed, had
> smitten with his fist Drum-Major Elzigood who, incensed
> at his own inaptitude, had threatened him with his cane.'

Wild Davy was David Haggart, who was to be hanged a
few hundred yards from that Rock eight years later. Borrow,
in the full flood of the Romantic imagination, went on to
couple him with Marlowe's Tamburlaine:

DAVID HAGGART

'Tamerlane and Haggart. Haggart and Tamerlane. Both these men were robbers, and of low birth, yet one perished on an ignoble scaffold, and the other died emperor of the world.'

The association, wild, even absurd, though it is, suggests Haggart's fascination for those connected with him. More heartfelt perhaps, though clumsy in expression, was to be the lament of a young girl who had been at school with him:

> O woe is me. What shall I say?
> Young David Haggart's gone.
> I did not think when at the school,
> He'd die a tree upon.
>
> Hail sober dullness! Ever hail!
> Young Haggart's at his rest.
> I hope he is enthron'd above
> And is for ever blest.

With its echo of the metrical Psalms this doggerel gives Haggart his due as the folk-hero he would have liked to be, and certainly sober dullness had little part in his brief life.

A less generous view was taken by his counsel, Henry Cockburn. Admitting that Haggart was 'young, good-looking, gay and amiable to the eye', he yet dismissed him with patrician contempt: 'there never was a riper scoundrel'. Even though there may be a certain indulgence in these words, they place Haggart firmly enough. He is set aside, shoved under; the Athenian balance is maintained, and Tamerlane is hardly a comparison likely to seem just to the judicious Whig. Any attempt to seek social significance in his short career would, we may suspect, receive even shorter shrift from his counsel. Professional criminals exist to be despatched, though the Law of course properly requires that they be adequately defended.

Tamerlane, the schoolboy fondly remembered, a ripe scoundrel: three views of young Haggart.

He was born in 1800 at Goldenacre, half-a-mile north of the old monastic mills on the Water of Leith. Within twenty years substantial bourgeois villas were being built there, but at that time it was still open country, and Haggart's father was a gamekeeper. Later he was to move to the south side of the Canongate, a district already in decline as the magnet of the New Town drew the middle classes away; there, declining himself, he set up as a dog-trainer. Haggart's own experience therefore was characteristic of the strongest trend in contemporary society, the move of the poor from country districts to the city.

Nevertheless he stands very much at this point of transition. He was a child of the Regency, and his world was a rumbustious one of race-meetings, stage-coaches, prizefights, wayside inns, gambling and flash coves. It was a world unsettled by twenty years of almost continuous war, a period of violent economic fluctuation, of an unprecedented movement of population, of sudden growth and equally sudden decline; a decade of booms and bankruptcies. Discharged soldiers wandered the countryside, the police were few and badly organised – in London the Metropolitan Police Force was not created till 1829, while in Edinburgh it was only in 1805 that a proper police force had superseded the old City Guard, whose picturesque appearance with their Lochaber axes was only surpassed by their total ineffectiveness.

The upper classes lived a life in which a polite formality strove to control innate exuberance. A strict code of manners was necessary because fierce passions were not far below the surface. The ultimate expression of this code was the duel, as it must be in a society where only fear of death will make people behave. Even politicians duelled; Castlereagh exchanged shots with Canning – and they were both Cabinet Ministers – while even Wellington called out a man who had libelled him. Such duels were rarely sanguinary; but you could never tell whether your opponent would be as restrained as you yourself intended to be. And duels were fought over trivial matters, the casual insult or the accusation of card-sharping, for example, at a time when gambling was the national passion. The purpose of the duel was clear: it preserved civil intercourse among equals. A savage penal code did the same thing for society as a whole. It existed to preserve property and to keep the lower classes in order.

It was necessary. We are too easily deceived by architecture and dress. As a result, admiring, for example, the dignity of Edinburgh's New Town, it is possible to forget social and political conditions, to forget the fragility of the Augustan social order. It was a violent and turbulent time. Edinburgh was growing fast – the population in 1811 was just over 100,000; ten years later it had increased to 138,235. This was a people ill to order, and the move of the middle classes away from the Old Town widened and deepened the gulf between rich and poor. In 1812, for example, there were riots on Hogmanay, which went some way beyond the traditional seasonal high spirits of Scotland's Saturnalia.

Towards midnight, the principal streets were taken possession of by gangs of young roughs from the lower parts of the town. They ran riot, armed with bludgeons. They attacked the police and overcame them for a time, and they knocked down and robbed many respectable citizens, taking their money, watches and hats. Two people were killed. Three youths, all under eighteen, were arrested and tried in March for their part in the affray. All were hanged in April. And all had Highland names – Hugh MacDonald, Hugh MacIntosh and Neil Sutherland.

Poor harvests could set the mob off. There were meal riots in the same year, and over six hundred people were also charged as professional beggars under the Vagrancy Acts. In 1813 a police constable was killed in a High Street riot, The turmoil and violence persisted for a good many years. Ian Campbell in his *Thomas Carlyle* (London, 1974) describes Edinburgh of the eighteen-twenties as being 'infested with hordes of mendicants' and quotes from a schoolboy's diary that there were 'crowds of thugs running after the people on the pavement, and striking them with their sticks and making a great noise.' As late as 1831 Lord Provost Allan was mobbed, stoned and forced to take refuge in a shop whence he had to be rescued by a company of dragoons despatched from the Castle. No doubt such events served to keep the authorities in touch with public opinion.

The most spectacular riot took place in 1818 and nothing more surely displays the fragility of the social order than this outbreak which was sparked off by the botched execution of Robert Johnstone. It was a shocking affair which provoked angry denunciations of the magistrates and the police. One onlooker, a student called William Macbean, described it in a letter to his mother as 'a second outbreak of the Porteous mob'; which mob Walter Scott described so powerfully in the same year in his novel *The Heart of Midlothian*.

Johnstone, an ignorant and stupid carter (these two qualities, ignorance and stupidity, not necessarily of course being found together) took to crime when thrown out of work by the depression that followed the end of the wars against Napoleon. His attempt at robbery was clumsy – his victim was easily able to make a confident identification, since Johnstone had obligingly elected to stage the assault immediately under a street-lamp. Although a case could be made for the unfortunate man – one defender wrote that he had associated with those, 'who were disposed to steal rather than to starve' – he was condemned to death, the Lord Justice-Clerk observing that, 'It was most lamentable that the severe example made, a few years back, of two young men of the same profession, for a crime exactly similar, should have had so little effect'. Doubtless he hoped that the repetition of the example would be more successful.

The execution, despite being attended, as was the custom, with all the pomp of civic dignity, was sadly bungled. It took place just outside St Giles, in the little open square formed by the church, the front of the Signet Library, the County Hall (described by a jaundiced onlooker as 'a wretched caricature of an Athenian temple') and the line of the High Street. Unfortunately the executioner was a novice and the drop had been miscalculated. Accordingly the miserable Johnstone hung there, being slowly strangled, with his toes still touching the table. Remedy was slow. The crowd, already sympathetic to Johnstone, whose colleagues in crime had escaped more easily, became restive. They realised that the man was still alive. 'Good God, the man's feet are not off the scaffold,' cried one. An attempt was made at rescue. The crowd rushed the platform, stones were thrown, and a young man, prompted, as Mr Macbean observed, 'by the impulse of humanity', cut down the body. The magistrate took prudent refuge in the church; the police likewise. Stones were now hurled at the windows. It was later claimed that as many as two hundred panes of glass were shattered.

Civis Edinesis took up the story in a letter to *The Scotsman*:

'A spectacle now presented itself which equalled in horror anything ever witnessed in Paris during the Revolution. The unhappy Johnstone, half-alive, stript of part of his clothes, and his shirt turned up, so that the whole of his naked back and upper part of his body was exhibited, lay extended on the ground in the middle of the street, in front of the police office. At last after some considerable interval, some of the police officers laying hold of the unhappy man, dragged him trailing along the ground, for about twenty paces into their den, which is also in the Old Cathedral . . .'

His ordeal had hardly run half its course. A surgeon bled him – to ascertain of course whether the wretch was still sufficiently alive to be hanged again. Reassured on this point, they prepared to resume. Meanwhile a magistrate had made his way to the Castle and called out the troops – the 88th Foot or Connaught Rangers under Major Grahame. When these had surrounded the scaffold and stood there with loaded muskets, it was considered safe to return to the hanging.

The half-naked Johnstone was led out. 'While a number of men were about him,' wrote *Civis Edinesis*, 'holding him on the table and fastening the rope about his neck, his clothes fell down in such a manner that decency would have been shocked had it been a spectacle of entertainment instead of an execution.'

Nor was this all. Johnstone next worked his hand free and tugged at the noose . . .

'The butchery continued until twenty-three minutes past four o'clock, long after the street lamps were lighted for the night, and the moon and stars distinctly visible . . .'

O Athens of the North.

Naturally there was criticism of the magistrates. It was splendidly said that they had shown 'contempt for the arbitrium popularis aurae.' Fortunately that noble body of men remained undisturbed in their complacency. They issued a statement superb in its bland self-exculpation:

'The magistrates', said the magistrates, 'not only employed a skilful tradesman to prepare the gibbet, but gave orders to the superintendent of Public Works to inspect it. Mr Bonnar did examine it, and reported to them that it was fit and suitable for the purpose intended. The charge that the Magistrates ought to have called out the city constables is ridiculous. Though there could be no anticipation of any attempt to interfere with the execution of the sentence of the law, no fewer than one hundred police officers were put upon actual duty and one hundred and thirty were in reserve. Thus every step that human prudence could devise was taken and the sentence of the law would have been executed in the usual manner, if a lawless mob had not stepped forward to prevent it, under pretence, as is now said, of showing humanity towards the criminal. The state of the fact is that notwithstanding the pains that had been taken to have the apparatus perfect, the rope was found to be too long, a fault alone imputable to the executioner, who had since been dismissed on that account.'

(It is interesting to observe that the simple action of checking the length of a rope evidently exceeds the limits of human prudence.)

'Hence, upon the criminal being thrown off, his toes touched slightly the drop below. This however was capable of being remedied in a few seconds; and the carpenters in attendance were immediately put upon that duty; and while in the act of removing the drop, the mob threw in a shower of stones and wounded several of them. The criminal also was wounded by one of the stones, to the effusion of his blood. The police officers endeavoured to preserve order,

15

but after several of them had been severely wounded, they were driven in upon the magistrates by the pressure of the very great and unusual multitude that had assembled; and the whole party was then forced into the adjoining church. Meantime part of the mob continued to throw stones and destroyed nearly two hundred panes of glass of the churches, while another party carried off the body of the criminal. The police officers in reserve, having now come forward, cleared the streets and got possession of the body, which was carried into the Police Office, where a surgeon, without any order from a magistrate, opened a vein . . . By this time one of the magistrates had gone to the castle, and had brought down a party of the military, and, the apparatus having been put up, it became the duty of the magistrates to carry the sentence into effect, and accordingly, within the period mentioned in the sentence, the criminal was again suspended, and hung till he was dead. Had the mob remained quiet, instead of offering a most daring outrage to the laws of their country, the criminal would have been dead in a few minutes after he was turned off. If therefore he has suffered more pain than the law intended, or if decency was in any way shocked by the appearance of the criminal when carried to and from the gibbet (and none can regret it more than the magistrates of the city) the blame alone rests with those who offered violence to the magistrates and their attendants.'

So, in tones that were to be familiar to succeeding generations of the Edinburgh citizenry, the magistrates recorded their entire satisfaction with their own performance; conscious virtue granted them a complete protection against any obloquy they might have attracted. And to cap it all, they offered a reward of fifty guineas for the apprehension of the young man who had cut down the body, though young Mr Macbean found it, 'difficult to say what crime he could be guilty of'; and they paid the Chief of Police, Captain Brown £100, 'for his great exertions at the execution', though *Civis Edinesis* denied that he had performed any such, alleging instead that he stayed 'sitting in his own room, in his own office, and though he had a reserve of between eighty and ninety of the best policemen in reserve in the Court Room, he remained inactive for between twenty and twenty five minutes, and never ventured to show his face till he was certain the military were on the ground. . . .'

The question of course, as always in such cases, suggests itself: was the riot in fact unpremeditated? The quantity of stones found ready to hand makes one wonder. At any rate, a city where the authorities were so unpopular and so supine could hardly be unhealthy or infertile for the criminal; as young David Haggart was to discover with delight.

Our main source of information about Haggart is inevitably suspect, for it is the autobiography he composed while under sentence of death in the Calton Jail. The sceptical Cockburn said that 'the confessions and the whole book were a tissue of absolute lies – and they had all one object – to make him appear a greater villain than he was'. Perhaps so; Cockburn had some direct knowledge of Haggart and rather more indirect knowledge of the world he had frequented. Perhaps, on the other hand, not; the Augustan contempt may here be a little too sweeping. Certainly Haggart's confession, though probably exaggerated in places and undoubtedly arranged to his advantage (but then whose autobiography isn't – even Cockburn's own *Memorials*?) yet paints a picture of the underworld that corresponds well enough with what we know from other sources. Haggart's own exploits may be exaggerated, but his world rings true enough. If he wasn't an honest autobiographer, then he was at least a novelist with something of the documentary authority of Defoe; and it would be in effect more remarkable to find this little book a work of the imagination than if it is what it purports to be, a memoir; albeit dressed up and improved in the telling.

The book deserves another comment too, before we pass to an account of Haggart's career, an account that will perforce continue to draw heavily on the autobiography, accepting it as by and large authentic. It is addressed to his solicitor and its purpose is plain enough; but there is no suggestion that he, or any other educated man, had a hand in the writing of it. Not even Cockburn seems to doubt Haggart's authorship, or find it surprising Yet surely it is strange enough. Haggart had no real schooling after the age of twelve or thirteen, and while he boasts that in his schooldays he was always dux in his class, one might expect that it was an achievement for one of his background to struggle into literacy. At the least one would expect his style to be clumsy and shapeless, but it is in fact admirably clear, direct, and sometimes even elegant. For example, his reflections on the effect of prison on young offenders are not only still to the point, but excellently expressed:

'A prison is the blackest and wickedest place in the world. Many a poor boy is brought to the gallows at last because his first offence is punished by imprisonment. This teaches him evil ways, whereas if he had been well flogged and sent home to his parents, he might have turned out a good man. I cannot say my bad habits were learned in jail, but I am sure they were confirmed there.'

There is an antithetical force in the last sentence of which Cockburn himself might not have been ashamed. If style is the man, it is not surprising that Haggart appears regularly to have made an engaging impression; that is how he writes also.

Apart from his boast of being dux, he says little about his schooldays, though he claims that he always satisfied his teachers. He probably knew how to do so; it is clear that he had charm enough, that most insidious of qualities which sets out, consciously or unconsciously, to disarm the moral judgement. He passes quickly to his first criminal exploits: the theft of a bantam hen from an old widow in Stockbridge, some shoplifting in the same district, and the rustling of a pony from a farmer in Currie to carry him and a friend home from a tiring country walk. None of these thefts was serious; none of them beyond the ordinary run of childish misdemeanour. They show little more than an adventurous spirit. Actually Haggart was not acquisitive. While under sentence of death, he was examined by a phrenologist, George Combe, who published his report and also, bound with it, the record of an interview with Haggart in which his findings were discussed. Its purpose was, in Combe's words, 'not to indulge in idle curiosity, but to throw light upon the natural dispositions which particularly lead a young man into a sporting kind of life'. Combe remarks defensively that, 'it has been conceived to be an anomaly in phrenology that Haggart should be addicted to stealing when the organ of acquisitiveness is only moderate in size'. He need not have felt the need for apology. The true thief – the thief of Haggart's stamp at least – is not greedy for possessions; he does not desire the object as an object, as a miser may desire gold, but rather as a means. It is what enables him to be true to the picture he has of himself.

David's childish pranks seem to have been easily forgiven. All that he has to say of his parents suggests that they were decent, loving people, always ready to forgive their errant son. No doubt he relied on that. All the same, domesticity was boring. Accordingly he enlisted as a drummer-boy in the Norfolk Militia, who were then (1813) stationed in Leith. The uniform attracted him and the promise of a varied life. Discipline however proved distasteful and he was happy to be discharged the following year, and to return to his father's home. Then followed a respectable interlude. He was apprenticed to Cockburn and Blair, millwrights and engineers, with whom he worked until the firm went bankrupt in 1817. He claims to have done well with them, to have enjoyed trust and responsibility: for instance he was allowed to carry money to and from the bank. Though one cannot resist the speculation of how his life might have developed if the firm had remained solvent, it is hard to imagine him content with dull respectability. The attractions of the sporting life, his image of himself as a fine fellow, would probably have proved too strong. At any rate, Cockburn and Blair's Bankruptcy threw him out of work in a year, when there were 1,600 unemployed workmen registered, and engaged by the Council in making the roads round the Calton Hill and the Salisbury Crags; impossible to imagine Davy Haggart as one of such a work-gang. In his own words, 'to work and be a slave to mankind. I could never think of'.

So, now that he was unemployed, he records that, 'in less

19

than three months I found myself plunged in such a state of vice and wickedness that my mind could not suffer reflection'. Perhaps so; more likely he thoroughly enjoyed it. His headlong gallop of a career had begun, as bitter-sweet as John Gay's Newgate Pastoral.

David Haggart had entered a world, 'where stealing was an activity so common as to be nothing less than banal'. The opportunities were legion, the pickings considerable and the chances of detection at least sufficiently long for the practitioner to discount them. David took to the streets, to casual shop-lifting and pickpocketing first. Probably nothing indicates the prevalence of theft so clearly as the extent of the thieves' cant in which they conversed. Whole paragraphs of Haggart's autobiography are completely incomprehensible without the aid of a glossary. 'Picking a suck' for instance, 'is a kittle job'; on the other hand 'the keek cloy is easily picked', and 'if blunt gets shy' you can always take to the 'hoys and coreing'. A 'prig' should keep an eye open for 'a coneish cove' and if he is 'well-budged', the job's easy. If you see a 'cove' with a 'lil' in his 'fam', then it should be yours, unless the 'topers' are to hand. Even readers steeped in the romances of Georgette Heyer will be baffled by the rich argot.

There was then a criminal underworld into which it was easy to sink. There were boozing-kens where a prig could lie up or houses of ill-fame where he would be hailed, Macheath-like, as a hero; and as for fencing the stuff, why Haggart sometimes found the choice embarrassing. He notes on one occasion that he couldn't recall where he had fenced some stolen goods, being drunk at the time. It must have seemed sometimes as if almost everything invited the young man to take up the sporting life. It was in those terms that he thought of it. Combe reports that, 'when we alluded to his crimes in common language, he became sullen and ceased to converse. He, however, used the phrase "the sporting line of life" himself; and we found that, on our employing it, he again became communicative.' It offered easy money, excitement and good living; 'the love of dress and company was my motive', he said. When the alternative was a choice between long laborious toil and starvation, it is not difficult to understand how a bright young spark like Davy Haggart should adopt the sporting line of life.

The first weeks of his new career are worth following in detail. They set the pattern for the rest of his short life. He was quickly established as a pickpocket, for which calling he showed a natural aptitude. 'I had the ill-luck to be born left-handed, and with thieves' fingers,' he remarks with the utmost complacency, 'for my forks were equally long, and they never failed me.' For one with these talents, race-meetings and country fairs, where people were free with their money, and often well-liquored, proved the natural habitat. Davy soon met with a young Irishman, Barney MacGuire, a few years older than himself, and experienced in the business. Barney and he became fast friends and partners.

In August they went together to Portobello Races, where they made £11. Determination of comparative money values is always difficult and frequently futile; both difficulty and futility are exacerbated when the society being considered shows very marked gradations in personal wealth. In the early nineteenth century the Earl of Durham could say, 'a man can jog along on £40,000 a year', while an agricultural labourer counted his week's wage in shillings. Captain Gronow in his incomparable *Reminiscences and Recollections* notes that, in the only hotel in London 'where you could get a genuine French dinner ... you would seldom pay less than three or four pounds; your bottle of champagne or of claret, in the year 1814, costing you a guinea.' Since Davy and Barney were aspiring to the High-Life rather than to mere subsistence, Gronow's figures may seem more relevant to their desires than a note on the price of bread.

The Portobello Races marked the start of a tour of the Borders and the North of England. They headed for Jedburgh and Kelso, where they cleared £20 at the St James's Fair, then to Hawick, where they stayed at the Black Bull, and thence, by way of Langholm, to Dumfries for the Rood Fair. For the boy until recently tied to his apprenticeship, respectability and labour, it was an exhilarating change of pace.

At Dumfries they stole £10 in a hosier's shop. David's own

21

description is a fair indication of their habitual effrontery. Having spied a man with who was seeking to change a ten pound note, he 'followed him into a hosier's shop in the High Street, where he again asked for change; the shop was throng and the shopman said he would give it presently. He put the note in a careless manner into his waistcoat pocket, when I was standing by him with my arms across, and in that position touched him of his scrieve (banknote). I immediately asked the shopman the price of silk stockings, which were in the window. His answer was "the price is marked on them, sir." This was the best answer in the world for me. I went out to see, but missed my way back. I did not inform young Mac-Guire of this prize; but Barney and I shared it with £4 of the smash taken by him.'

Young MacGuire was Barney's brother, who had recently joined them. The relations between David and Barney may be fairly judged by their exclusion of the young MacGuire from a share in the profits. They were both ready to cheat their confederates, but David was also prepared to take risks on Barney's behalf. His tone is warm and sincere whenever he speaks of him; David and Jonathan also ran.

Dumfries was dangerous however, because of Barney's record. 'We were not in safety to be seen at this place, as the MacGuires were well-known by John Richardson (a most respectable sheriff-officer from Dumfries) whom we suspected was at the Fair.' Richardson flits through David's story, one of those persistent, dogged detectives one meets in nineteenth century novels: like Wilkie Collins' Sergeant Cuff, or Inspector Bucket in *Bleak House*, he had no method but a terrier's. His presence was sufficiently alarming however to persuade Barney to keep to their inn room. Despite this, there were good pickings at Dumfries: Davy got £23 off a drunken farmer. (Such unhappy men were among his most frequent victims. Indeed if other pickpockets met with comparable success, as seems likely, the phrase 'agricultural depression' takes on a new meaning. Bad harvests were not necessarily the worst of it.)

Langholm Fair, whither they next proceeded, was to provide one of their most notable coups. Young MacGuire spotted their chosen victim – 'a coneish cove (gentleman) with a great swell in his suck. He had seen him with the lil in his fam. and he was sure there were hundreds in it'. It was an opportunity not to be let slip. Davy went to it with a will and admirable speed of hand. He got £201, and they cheated young MacGuire of his fair share yet again. This was indeed the life. 'I never was happier in my life than when I fingered all this money; but I thought about it sore afterwards when I was ill and like to die.' Such repentance, brief when it came, cast no shadow on present pleasure. However within half an hour of the coup, they saw the persistent Richardson 'running about'. It was time to be off; nothing after all could explain their wealth but the truth. Fortunately it enabled them to travel like gentry. They ordered a post-chaise and set off for Carlisle.

There followed the sort of interlude that was the reward of their profession; four weeks in which they could live like the bucks, swells or dandies they saw themselves as being. They passed the mornings riding, their afternoons and evenings gaming and occasionally took in a dance. It was a provincial version of the life led by their social superiors, the Corinthians themselves. Barney of course was a dab hand at all this, an 'excellent card-player', Davy assures us; 'to him I am indebted for the great proficiency I afterwards arrived at in the use of cards, dice or billiards.' But unlike the gentry they aped, Barney and David were businessmen, with a calling to follow. Money soon ran through their hands. Stocks had to be replenished. Pleasure, the criminal soon realises, has to be paid for. This time they received a check, the first of young David's career. An attempted 'snib' in the Rickergate failed. Worse, they aroused the suspicion of the authorities, who must always have kept a wary eye on such newcomers to the town as flashed money about, had no obvious source of income, did no work, and could not – whatever their pretensions – qualify as gentry. Barney and David found that the constables had taken possession of their portmanteaux and awaited them at their inn. No doubt they were to be asked to assist with inquiries. It was a distasteful notion and they were naturally reluctant; it was time to evaporate. They did so, making no effort to salvage their goods. Easy come, after all, easy go. They left town at once, pausing only to replenish their wardrobes, 'bilking and fleecing a merchant-tailor'.

Next stop was Kendal Fair, 'one of the finest horse-markets in England'. Here a 'deeker' attempted to queer their pitch. Much to their irritation, they found themselves compelled to pose as bona fide horse dealers, and even buy a horse to divert suspicion from their real activities. They sold it almost at once. Less skilled in this sort of business than in their chosen avocation, they dropped five shillings on the deal. The loss was short-lived. Reverting to their proper role, they then robbed the buyer and found themselves in the end £43 to the good. Continuing their round of the Northern Fairs they proceeded to Morpeth, where they found a deal of criminal competition, but where the resourceful Barney fleeced a gang of prigs from York.

They felt entitled again to the reward of leisure, and established themselves in Newcastle, taking private lodgings in Castle Street as John Wilson and James Atkinson, gentlemen travelling for pleasure. Their standing was evident, at least in their own eyes: 'great swells with our white-caped coats. top boots and whips'. The landlady had three daughters, 'very pleasant girls', says David complacently, and with them they passed 'a jolly Christmas Day, 1817'.

He had been in business just eight months.

One night in the New Year they took the girls to the theatre, where Barney, more experienced and always mindful that they had to work in order to continue to live in their chosen style, proposed a theft. David replied that, 'it might be done if it were not for the blones' (girls). It was therefore agreed that he should occupy them while Barney lifted the loot. It was worth £70, but this did not defray their Newcastle expenses by £14. They therefore resorted to burglary, a new departure for David but not for Barney. In the course of the job they tied up the master of the house, but burglary had dangers that their normal pursuits lacked. Unless a pickpocket is actually identified in the instant he commits his crime, or found with the stuff on him, detection is difficult; all that can usually be said is that he was in the crowd, in the vicinity. And the nature of a crowd is such that this can be said of many

others. Burglary however admits to a more positive identification, especially when you have had to tie up witnesses.
David and Barney were both apprehended within days. 'Unfortunately,' says David (rashly or stupidly, one may rather
think) they were wearing the same clothes in which they had
committed the burglary. They were carried off to Durham,
tried and returned to prison to await sentence of death at the
end of the assizes.

Fortunately early nineteenth century jails were not so hard
to escape from. The buildings were frequently old and in poor
repair, the turnkeys aged also, drunken, corrupt and incompetent. Barney, David and some other prisoners in the same
unhappy condition set to work on the wall of their cell. Interrupted by a turnkey, whose slumbers the noise had disturbed,
they seized him, 'took the dubs, and bound and gagged him'.
They gained the backyard and scaled the wall. By bad luck
Barney and another prisoner fell back after reaching the top,
and, the hue and cry having been raised, were recaptured.

Here however the amiable element of David's character
reveals itself. He at once organised Barney's escape. It would
have been easy to have shrugged his shoulders and said, 'well,
that's the way of the world'. Not at all; at some personal risk
he got him out, perhaps killing of a policeman in the course of
the action. 'Whether I have his murder to answer for, I cannot
tell, but I fear my aim was true and the poor fellow looked
dead enough.' If so, it probably sat lightly enough on his conscience. It is difficult to place much value on another's life,
when you hold your own cheap.

The escape was vain enough, for after another tour of the
Borders, Barney was again arrested. Still legal liaison was so
poor that he was not identified as the perpetrator of the
Durham burglary, who should have been awaiting sentence
of death, and in fact he received only three months' imprisonment. The disconsolate David returned to Newcastle and his
old lodgings, where he amused himself with his worthy landlady's daughters, and did not work till the Spring, 'having
been tolerably successful in gambling'. This association in
Newcastle appears to have been the only respectable one of his
adult life. Pleasant though it was, it provided in its cosy and

25

DAVID HAGGART

teasing domesticity, no substitute for the glamour and thrills of action. In the early summer of 1818 David returned to Edinburgh.

Naturally he found lodgings in the Old Town, first on the south side of the Grassmarket. He was now a fully – fledged member of his profession, and as such was quickly absorbed in a dense yet multifarious, fraternity. The rhythm of his life was established. It was one of short stops and sudden aid to identification. There must have been many who knew Haggart well enough. Edinburgh was still a small city, even more so in geography than in population – and the handsome red-headed boy, still only eighteen, was not someone easily ignored. Yet the fraternity could absorb him easily. There was nothing fixed or formal about it of course; it had no limits. The cheap lodging-house, the boozing ken and the brothel were not easily distinguished from each other; they were all part of David's world, a world where he had also innumerable associates and casual partners. One example will suffice, his encounter one day with George Bagrie and William Paterson, a fortuitous meeting which reveals very clearly something of the nature of their society. They were, in David's disdainful words, 'very willing but poor snibs'. David came upon them when they were with 'a lushy cove' on whom they were going to work 'in a very feckless manner'. Irritated by their evident incompetence – perhaps they were a spot lushy themselves, always an occupational hazard when so much time was spent waiting for prospective victims to attain a suitable state of inebriation – he intervened, carried out the job on their behalf, and then proceeded with them to a house on South Bridge, kept by Miss Gray, a celebrated Madame; for refreshment of one kind, or several.

These crimes were all small beer, pickpocketing or shoplifting for the most part. There was always a market for watches and clothes, and numerous fences ready to accommodate the thief, who was thus spared the embarrassment of having the goods long in his possession. David was wise enough to ring the changes of his fences. It was a mistake – as admirers of *The Beggar's Opera* will be aware – for the thief to put himself in the power of a fence, who might find it expedient to shop him.

Normally the fence would pay about 25% of the value of goods. David stole surprisingly often from drapers and hosiers, and not merely when he wanted something nice to give a girl, but as a matter of policy. There was clearly a good demand for the stuff. This is something the thief soon learns: to take what will find a ready market. In this respect he is a businessman like any other. No more point in stealing what is out of fashion than in writing five act tragedies in blank verse; in neither case will it go. Among the fences David used were Billy Cook in the Calton (just below the Jail) and John Johnstone in Crosscauseway. There were a good many Johnstones or Johnstons, apart from the unfortunate twice-hanged Robert, engaged in criminal activities in the city at that time; it was as if the Border reivers had moved north and retained their old morality. Davy lodged with one for a bit, and had at another time a girl-friend called Jean Johnston, with whom, in one of his less credible stories, he claimed once to have effected the release of some prisoners: 'went to the lock-up shop, and having plied the keeper with plenty of budge, I took the key and let out six of the prisoners'.

As a diversion from city life, there were trips out of town, to the autumn races at Perth for example. The morning coach from Princes Street allowed the traveller to do the journey in less than a day, arriving in Perth about four in the afternoon. Perth was a good town for the profession, as traditional border towns usually are, and David found farmers, venturing south of the Highland Line, regular prey. It was a good centre too for day trips to local fairs – Dunkeld and Kenmore for instance – and for visits to Dundee and longer trips up the coast, as far as Aberdeen. It became in fact his second Scottish home. Whenever he felt bored, or perhaps a bit closely over-watched in Edinburgh, he took a little trip to Perth. It was there he once, with his friend Dr Black, agreeably lightened the punishment that some colleagues in the fraternity were due to receive. These wretches had been sentenced to be whipped through the town ('coored through the voil' in Haggart's cant – clearly French-derived, this expression). The Doctor, a burly and resouceful criminal, joined with David in getting hold of the hangman whose job it was to lay on the whip. They plied him with liquor and then threatened him that 'if he was severe on them, we would darken him'. It is the old technique, familiar from a hundred B Feature movies: soften 'em up, treat 'em rough.

There were always good friends in Perth. Towards the end of his career, when his luck seemed to be running out, he could still find safety there. Approached in his lodgings once, he was able to fob off the police by adopting a high tone, which his landlord was happy to support. 'What's your name?' 'That's a very rude question to ask of any gentleman.' If he is to be believed – and it must be confessed that this is one story where Reason prompts agreement with Cockburn's scepticism – this was sufficient to check the police; David's landlord then assured them that he was a respectable gentleman who always paid his bills in time (as of course prudent criminals do, at least in the right quarters), and the atmosphere became sufficiently relaxed to allow him to slip out of the back door to 'one of the most profligate houses in town', where naturally he was perfectly safe, and remained till it was time to resume business at Glamis Fair.

He had his odd moments of repentance, generally when in poor health. Then he would promise his parents to remain with them and resume trade. The promises were made in faith and sincerity. Only somehow, when the fear of death receded, his naturally blithe spirit re-asserted itself; the contrast between drab respectability and the pleasures and excitement of the sporting life was too marked. 'When I recovered, all thoughts of repentance soon left my mind.' Still, for a time at least, it was useful to have parents who could provide a base for convalescence and a respectable alibi also. This is something professional criminals are usually swift to learn: the value of safe houses.

David however was too full of levity to set a proper value on this, just as he soon neglected the old rule that the fox does not rob in his own backyard. Instead he worked harder and faster in Edinburgh and Leith than anywhere else. In February 1820 for example he committed ten crimes in eight days in Leith; no wonder that he should have decided that the town was 'a pretty good place for a few adventures'. His speciality there was housebreaking. 'I generally entered the houses in Leith by forcing in the small window above the outer doors. This was an invention of my own, but it is now so common that I mention it to put families on their guard.'

His rate of criminal activity was so great that his luck was bound to run out. Captain Ross of the Leith Police had his eye on him. No doubt there was somebody ready to inform. In those days, before the arrival of scientific aids to detection, the police were even more dependent on informers than they are now. Captain Brown of the Edinburgh Police made this quite clear, defending his establishment of a secret fund to buy information. Few criminals indeed would have been convicted – only those caught red-handed or with the proceeds of their robbery on them – but for the existence of this useful and despised body of men.

Ross and his constables apprehended Haggart in his lodgings in Johnston Street, North Leith. He put up a struggle, and is kind enough in his Memoirs to commend the 'humanity' displayed by Sergeant Thorn in the course of the arrest. Haggart's career shows clearly enough how police and criminals had, and still have, much in common. It wasn't only in fiction that thief-catchers and thieves talked the same language, a language that often excluded those not immediately concerned with criminal activity. And Haggart kept meeting the same policemen – Captain Brown and Ross as well as the persistent John Richardson. Clearly they had also numerous acquaintance in common who were ready enough to tip either side the wink, as seemed most expedient.

This time however David broke out of Leith Jail and immediately 'went upon the hoys and got about twelve yards of superfine blue cloth'. This wasn't the foolish or incorrigible act it might first appear. David had resolved prudently to get out of Edinburgh for a time; the journey had to be financed, and there was no other means of doing so. He was off to the Borders again, heading for Dumfries by way of a cattle show at Kelso. In Dumfries he was delighted to come upon Barney again, but his time the joy was short-lived, Barney being snatched by the ubiquitous and tireless Richardson. His luck was finally exhausted. He got, 'a free passage to Botany Bay for a fourteen stretch. He was a choice spirit and a good friend to me. We spent many a joyous merry hour together, for I had no thought and no sorrow till I lost Barney.' The elegaic note is irresistible.

The pace could not last. David himself was soon captured again, and had no longer the advantage of anonymity. Instead he had risen to the status of a wanted man. This time he could not hope for a mere brief spell of imprisonment such as an earlier one when Captain Brown had sent him to The Planting for four months. (He had been put in charge of the young prisoners there – 'I had a rope for punishing them and I never spared the use of it', he records, a note which does credit to his honesty (or lack of imagination) rather than his humanity). This time they were determined to make an end of him; deal with him once and for all. He had become a well-known nuisance. He was committed to the Calton Jail, and indicted to stand trial at the High Court of Justiciary for one act of housebreaking, eleven acts of theft and one act of prison breaking. He admitted his guilt, having no hope of acquittal, but with some optimism: the admission might mitigate his sentence. However, as it happened, there were still more charges to answer and he was indicted to stand trial at the next Dumfries Circuit, for the business in which he had been concerned there. The bills were coming in.

He tried to escape on the way, but was foiled. Not despairing however, he determined to break jail. He did not anticipate difficulty. He made his plans, and had everything in hand for an escape on his own, when other prisoners, with similar ideas in mind, involved him in their plan. As he grandly remarks, 'having thus, as I thought, secured my own liberty, by getting everything ready for a start, in a way which none could prevent. I was too easily engaged in another scheme with Dunbar. As I considered myself safe, I did not much care whether we succeeded or not; but I thought it would be a fine thing to make a clean sweep of the quoad (jail)'.

This was either conceit or sheer good-nature, either way, it was a fatal decision. His associates' plan was simple in the extreme. They would get hold of a stone, tie it up in a cloth, and strike the turnkey on the head. They would then find it easy to remove the keys and release all the prisoners. No plan could more completely expose the rudimentary security system of Regency jails. It was of course preposterous; nothing so elementary could possibly work; there must, one would think, have been some other precautions. One would be wrong; there weren't and it did.

It was an ill success for David. He had deplored the plan, originally saying that, if he should get his liberty, he would never strike the sergeant or turnkey for it. Nevertheless it was David who held the bag with the stone, David who struck the turnkey (the sergeant had gone to the Races), David who rifled the key, David in short who led the escape. Vanity and conceit forbade him to take second place, even in a plan, not of his devising, which was supplanting a far safer one of his own. One can only conclude that to some extent he willed his own destruction.

For such it was to be. By ill luck, almost certainly not by design, the turnkey was killed. With one blow David had advanced his status from petty thief and pickpocket to killer. The tenacious Richardson, in whose territory the crime had been committed, resolved to hunt him down.

A note of panic enters David's account. For the first time, it seems, he felt the danger and isolation of his position. Henceforth, he is no longer in charge of his life; he is a marked man; as much the hunted as the hunter. It was not of course the consciousness of guilt that made the change. True, he affects a pity for the wretched turnkey, and a regret for the deed, that contrast strongly with the nonchalance with which he described the possible killing of a policeman in the Durham escape. Yet the real pity is not directed outwards, but at himself. He is shocked by the realisation that a moment's unthinking and quite avoidable action should have brought him to this pitch. He was learning what the criminal mind would always prefer to ignore: that actions have consequences.

He was on the run now, twisting and turning like a hare, knowing that every man, even members of the fraternity, was ready to turn him in. (Perhaps the qualification should be withdrawn; murderers are always regarded as bad news in criminal circles, if only because they stimulate police activity.) Dumfries, Carlisle, Newcastle, he twisted his way along the Border. He determined to return to Scotland, 'as I knew they would never suspect me of going there, where I was so well known', he says, displaying the same fallacious cleversilly reasoning that Poe exhibited in *The Purloined Letter*. It is rarely as intelligent to do the obvious in the expectation that the obvious will not be anticipated as ingenious criminals may imagine. The police, stolid rather than inspired, will competently cover the obvious. A criminal's bolt-holes will not escape investigation because of some fanciful theory that they are too well known for him to use. Something of this may have occurred to David, for, uncertain of his logic, he hesitated a week in Berwick, during which time he watched the arrival of the Edinburgh coaches, his eye wary for police officers. Finding none arrive, he resolved to return to Edinburgh itself. It was after all home, the burrow towards which the instinct of the hunted animal directed him.

He travelled thither with Mr Wipers whom he met at Dunbar. Mr Wipers, a stranger to the city and with no acquaintance there, took a fancy to Davy and importuned him with requests for his company. He pressed him with invitations for walks, for the theatre, for tavern evenings; but, 'I always pretended to be unwell'. Mr Wipers persisted. Eventually Davy gave way – possibly Mr Wipers was asking awkward questions, possibly David was bored. He continued however to exercise unwonted prudence and selected Mrs Mackinnon's on South Bridge as their rendezvous, notorious as the livelist of the city's numerous houses of ill-fame. Mrs Mackinnon herself was to follow Davy to the scaffold within a few years for stabbing an officer whose custom had proved unsatisfactory. It was therefore a house where Davy could feel safe among friends, even in his unprecedentedly nervous condition.

It passed off smoothly, without incident. Mr Wipers left the city, but David continued to lie low, quitting his lodgings only by night, and even then, in the additional security of female disguise. On one such expedition he encountered his poor father who failed to recognize his son dressed in 'blones' twigs'. No doubt that was just as well; there was enough to distress him already.

Still such caution becomes wearisome. David was soon able to convince himself that the chase was cooling. It was after all inconvenient and boring to live like this. It was surely safe to resume the normal course. Such self-deception, allowing 'what would be' to represent 'what is', is common enough of course; it is though a habit of thought to which the criminal mind, with its inherent tendency to solipsism, is peculiarly given.

David however was soon disillusioned.

He made a visit – a business visit of course, for a criminal must steal to live – to his old haunts in Leith. There he was unlucky enough – yet it was of course the sort of luck that might, in the circumstances have been anticipated – to come face to face with old adversary, Captain Ross. They were no more than ten yards apart. 'Mustering up my pluck, I plunged my fam into my suck' (my hand into my pocket), as if for a pop (a gun). The cautious Captain, who knew me too well to engage me while alone, took to his heels.'

It would be interesting to have Captain Ross's version; yet Davy's, Walter Mittyish though it certainly is, could be true enough. At any rate this encounter, or some similar alarm, was enough to persuade him it was time to get out again. Now that he was positively known to be back in Edinburgh, nowhere in the city was safe. It is doubtful if the wretched boy had anyone he could rely on; it was too late to go back to his parents. Those days, when their home could afford sanctuary, were over. He had advanced beyond being a suspicious character whom the law would like to keep an eye on; instead he was well and truly on the run.

He made for Fife at once, taking a passage in a fishing-boat from Fisherrow and landing at Siller-Dykes (the modern Cellardyke, a village which adjoins Anstruther.) His movements were agitated and apparently random. He headed for Dundee, where he robbed a jeweller and picked a pocket in a crowd, thence to Cupar, Kinghorn, Burntisland and back to Newhaven and Edinburgh. He lacked a base, could only keep moving and moved without purpose. There was nowhere as dangerous as Edinburgh; yet 'I could not keep myself away'.

DAVID HAGGART

Even the autobiography can hardly hide his agitation. What was he to do?

The first thing he saw on return was a bill posted, which offered a reward of seventy guineas for his apprehension. Once he might have been flattered. Now the thought uppermost in his mind was the realisation that none of his many acquaintances in the city could be trusted not to shop him for that price. Safe houses were a thing of the past.

Leith – Kinghorn – Dundee – Perth – the journeyings were resumed. There was at least safety of mind in movement; anything was better than waiting. And of course there was work to be done. He found Perth illuminated for the Queen's acquittal; that offered good pickings, and there is an appropriate irony in Davy, this characteristic figure of the Regency underworld, feeding off a crowd which had assembled to proclaim their detestation of the Regent who was now George IV.

For a few weeks he resumed his old style of life, though fear was ever with him and the old blitheness was never quite recaptured. There were no more periods of idleness and fine living. Dunkeld – Perth – Dundee – Kenmore Fair – Cupar Fair – Arbroath Fair and back to Perth again. A little bit of business here, a little bit there. Now came the moment already referred to when he only just escaped capture in his Perth lodgings. The change in his style of life, the acceleration of his movements, suggests what one might surmise without any evidence: that, as a wanted man, he was having to pay more for his lodgings, to buy even the most temporary and short-lived security.

Even so, there were good moments, an exploit at Glamis Fair for example, which reads like a comic opera dry run for one of the most celebrated incidents in Stevenson's '*Weir of Hermiston*.'

'Towards evening I spied a farmer plank a run lay of screaves in his keek cloy and I determined to have them if possible. I soon after saw him mount his prad, and watching the way he went, I immediately got my prad and followed him, accompanied by Edgy mounted behind me and

a snib, named Smith, on foot. On getting up with the
farmer, we found that other two had joined him. Smith
objected to make an attack, Edgy joined him. . . . Having
parted with these cowards, I followed up my prey, and I
soon observed my man stop to water his horse at a small
burn; I got alongside of him, and very unceremoniously
plunged into his keek cloy and brought the blunt up with
me, and before he had time to challenge me, I hit him a very
smart blow over the head with the butt end of my whip,
which set him off at full gallop and I at no less . . .'

Action could still drive out anxiety, but the course could
not last. A new departure was necessary, and a trip to Glasgow suggested the answer: he might give Ireland a go.

The crossing was not entirely without incident. He was a
little disturbed to find himself being regarded with suspicion
by one of the passengers, who turned out to be Provost Fergus
of Kirkcaldy. The Provost had almost certainly seen the
posters and it is a little surprising that he contented himself
with staring. Possibly he had urgent business and knew how
any attempt to assist the police could cause delay. At any rate
he did nothing and Davy had another temporary reprieve.

Ireland restored his spirits at once. In those days, long
before the great famine of the eighteen-forties, it seemed a
bustling go-ahead place, with, significantly, more to offer a
lad of his profession than Scotland had. 'Paddyland', he says,
'is the land for pickpockets, lots of money, oceans of drink' (it
is of course so much easier to rob a man well in liquor than one
soberly vigilant and knocking-down pell-mell – then is the
time to work away at the business. England is too much
hunted, and there is no money in Scotland'.

He embarked therefore on a wild fling of crime and revelry
that took him on a mad gallop through the country. Yet all the
time he was in Ireland the hunt was catching up on him, for
the worthy Provost Fergus had indeed had second thoughts,
and had written to Dumfries reporting his suspicions, a
method of procedure that had the advantage for him of dis-
rupting his own activities not at all. David could only reflect
later that it had been a fortunate means of proceeding for the

DAVID HAGGART

Provost. 'It was well for me that I did not know his suspicions at the time, for he went on shore in black night, and I could easily have put him under the wave.' Well for the Provost too. Still the information thus laid took time to catch up, and Davy was able to enjoy his revelry in his fools' paradise.

He robbed pig drovers and gamblers, losing on one occasion a hundred pounds because he was too careless to search a bundle of letters properly. He survived information laid against him by one Robert Platt, formerly an inmate of Dumfries. He was posted in the Dublin paper *Hue and Cry*, spent £190 on a month's trip with a couple of girls by jaunting-car through Fermanagh, Cavan and Derry, moved between Dublin and Belfast following the fairs and race-meetings, was arrested and released, beat up a police spy and was himself attacked by a pig drover brandishing a shillelagh – he showed great energy in exacting an apology from this man. All in all he lived a violent, crowded, helter-skelter life; there could be no doubt that the pace was hotter in Ireland, where the drink flowed even more freely than in Scotland and where every man was quick to pull a shillelagh to avenge a fancied insult.

Still, David resolved to move on, first to France, then perhaps to America. However, when on the point of taking his passage, he heard of a fair to be held the next day at Clough. Inevitably, he 'resolved to attend and practise my profession for the last time in the British dominions.' An ill-fated resolve; he was arrested on a charge of picking a pocket, and confined in Downpatrick jail.

At first this was not too bad. There was soon a prison riot. They broke through to the women's quarters and barricaded themselves in, indulging for three days in an orgy that in retrospect shocked even David. At last the authorities restored order and David was brought to trial. It gave him a poor opinion of Irish justice. 'I have been twice tried for my life in Scotland', he wrote. 'The first time I got more than justice, for I was acquitted. The second time I got justice, for I was convicted. But in Ireland I got no justice at all; for at Downpatrick there was none to speak for me but the Judge, and he spoke against me.'

Be that as it may, he was remanded to Kilmainham Jail, where his opinion of Irish justice did not improve. There were two beautiful girls there, murderesses, and, when with innocent and sunny good nature. David attempted to speak some words of comfort to them, he found himself clapped in an iron helmet, so constructed that he could not move his tongue and was therefore constrained in silence. It was not what he was accustomed to, not this life of waiting, with nothing to do but contemplate the antics of an insane prisoner, condemned for having skinned a horse alive.

At last the purpose of the delay was made clear. Looking out of his cell window he saw John Richardson cross the yard. The information laid by Provost Fergus had done its work. David's number was up. Obstinately he refused at first to face the facts, maintaining his Irish identity and denying that he had ever been in Scotland. It was all in vain. Richardson knew him too well to be deceived, and was determined that this time his prey should not escape. Elaborate precautions were taken to guard against this possibility on the return journey.

'An iron belt was fixed round my waist, with my wrists pinioned to each side of it; a chain passed from the front of the belt and joined the centre of a chain, each end of which was padlocked round my ankle, and a chain passed from each wrist to each ankle.' Trussed like this, he admitted the truth. He found himself 'fed like a sucking turkey in bedlam and treated like a helpless infant.' Richardson and the Law had won. All the same he was still prepared to make things difficult if he could. 'They could not get what they call a declaration out of me, for I knew that would be used against me, so I thought it as well to keep my tongue within my teeth, and this I would advise every man who is accused of crime to do, whether he is innocent or guilty.'

All the same this was strictly a matter of self-respect, nothing more. From the moment of his arrest and return from Ireland his fate was certain. There was nothing he could hope for. All that was left him was to put on a good show. He had to live up to the image he held of himself, which he wished others to retain. That desire was by no means ignoble; reputation was a

37

matter of pride, and he had nothing else to leave.

'During the trial', reported the *Caledonian Mercury*, 'he preserved the greatest composure, while his Lordship addressed him, he leaned back on the seat in a careless attitude, at the same time eating confections; but when called upon to attend to the sentence, he stood erect and heard it unmoved.'

Idly eating confections – that showed the dandy touch, Brummell in the bow window of White's; also the ability to regard events even of this importance with admirable detachment. The composure with which he received the sentence demonstrated imperturbability, the capacity to take it, which the eighteenth century called 'bottom', and admired greatly.

It wasn't, as such imperturbability might easily be, evidence of insensibility. Haggart was no dumb animal, nor one inarticulate in suffering. On the contrary it was the result of a highly conscious exercise of self-control. 'They say I looked careless, but they could not see within me', he noted.

Now all that remained was to set himself right with this world and prepare for death. He worked at his autobiography, his *apologia pro vita sua*; it was all he had to offer the world, for his estimated profit of £912 on his four years' trading was quite dissipated. The purpose of the autobiography was then usual enough, whether one accepts Cockburn's strictures or not. He wanted to leave some record of himself that would establish his life as having had a certain sort of significance; it was intolerable to think that he could simply evaporate.

It had been a life consumed in activity, a hectic pell-mell of succession of incidents that all served no purpose beyond the gratification of the moment. The autobiography may be read as an attempt, slight, desperate, but in its way gallant, to extract some meaning from it all; probably this explanation is at least as accurate as Cockburn's. There is in the end not so great a difference in certain important respects between the criminal and his advocate as the latter would have us believe. Both feel their evanescence; both experience a need to impose some order on their existence; both turn to the autobiographical mode.

For the same reason David endured the phrenologist,

George Combe, a man, like many enthusiasts, of little humour and no wit. His visits did not only serve to pass the time in the condemned cell, a place, one must assume, where any unoccupied time possesses a frightening duality: it hangs heavy and is yet filled with a horrid apprehension of its brevity. Combe's enquiry however promised David something more: either the chance to understand himself more fully, or at least a reinforcement of what he already believed. Nobody now accepts phrenology as a science, but it was so considered by many at the time: the reflection may serve as a warning for those enamoured of contemporary modes of pseudo-science.

David was indignant and quick to correct Combe when he made mistakes. For instance Combe found that the indications of sexuality were low. Naturally David was ready with denial. On the contrary his enthusiasm for the girls was, 'one of the causes of my downfall'. Perhaps so; on the other hand, like many men of action, he never formed a lasting connection, indication perhaps of the inability to experience any deep passion. There were touches of Don Juan about David, and the classical Don Juan is a Narcissist who uses women partly as decoration, partly to feed his sense of power. He can never make the surrender of self which the true capacity to love demands; so, even in company, he is essentially alone, imprisoned in his excessive egoism. Of course David never attained maturity; not many young men, even those of more settled occupation, do form lasting connections between the ages of seventeen and twenty-one. One must remember that his exploits were those of a young blade, whose character was unformed. Certainly his only deep recorded attachment was to Barney MacGuire, and that clearly partook of hero-worship, an adolescent emotion. Barney was his mentor, as well as his *fidus Achates*. No one replaced him. After Barney's disappearance David was on his own.

Combe found that David's greatest errors had, 'arisen from a great self-esteem, a large combativeness, a prodigious firmness, a great secretiveness'. No doubt there is something in all this, though one's confidence in Combe's judgement, already perhaps impaired by doubts as to his method, is reduced by his subsequent observation that Haggart's cunning appears, not only in his crimes, his escapes, and his deceptions, but in his refusing to emit a declaration before trial. To equate common sense with cunning is to exhibit a naive inclination for melodrama and hyperbole.

In fact Haggart's course, which Combe describes as his 'errors', is easily enough accounted for. There were only two means by which he might rise from his position in society: industry and crime. And he was averse to work. A young man of ambition but no fortune has a limited choice. If his tastes run to excitement and high living, his course is likely to be set; the sporting life is there to beckon invitingly. David Haggart was by no means remarkable; plenty of young sparks followed the same sort of career, even though they lacked his intelligence, charm and verve.

Combe went on to compare him to other murders, such as Bellingham who assassinated the Prime Minister, Spencer Perceval in 1812. The comparison was more or less pointless. Haggart was in no way deranged like Bellingham, and he was not even, in one very real sense, a murderer. No one has ever suggested that he intended to kill the unfortunate turnkey. He merely hit out at someone who happened to stand in his way, and we may even believe him when he expresses his distress. He cannot be compared with the other murderer's temperament, which can well exist, as in William Bennison and more celebrated examples such as Major Armstrong, among those who are otherwise law-abiding and even see themselves as virtuous members of society. David Haggart belongs to a different, perhaps more numerous, category; that of the professional criminal who kills in a moment of desperation or carelessness. It is true of course that any distinction between murderers and other criminals is far from clear, and can easily be pushed too far. Often it may be no more than an expression of degree. All criminals, after all, have an excessive idea of their own importance, of their individuality; they are not prepared to adjust themselves to social norms which interfere with their self-expression. Murder may be interpreted as the extreme statement of the ego, expressing a willingness to obliterate anyone whose existence constitutes an obstacle to the ego's gratification. The murderer reduces all life to a point where it must submit to his will.

Popular opinion has always been accustomed to make a distinction between murder and other crimes. Difference of degree comes to represent difference in kind, if it is pushed far enough. To take another man's property is seen to be one thing; offensive certainly to the laws of man. To take his life is quite another thing, a crime which has entered a different dimension, an offence against the laws of God.

It was to these that David, condemned by the laws of Man, had now to prepare to submit himself. Those condemned to death had not only the gallows to confront; from the moment sentence was pronounced they were besieged by the clergy. The ministers were doing nothing but their duty; they had souls to save. It would be impertinent to question their sincerity. To face a man doomed to die in a few days must always arouse feelings of awe. It is not however cynical to observe that it also offers an unrivalled opportunity. As Dr. Johnson remarked, 'when a man knows he is to die in a fortnight, it concentrates his mind wonderfully'. In these circumstances the ministers went to work with a will.

Notable success had been achieved in the case of the three young men who were hanged after the 1812 riots. All had admitted their previous ignorance of, or indifference to, religion. All had been converted and had died with Bibles in their hands, proclaiming their faith that they were going to meet their God. Clearly, at the very least, the ministers' intervention performed a useful service. It gave the condemned men the courage to die with dignity, and that suited the authorities, for it awed the crowd and convinced them of the terrible majesty of the law. The Rev Mr Porteous, who spent many hours with them after their sentence, published a little book recounting their conversion. He expressed the hope that it would be an inspiration to others; that they would learn from it to lead a godly life and eschew temptation; but the others had not been sentenced to death, and so, for the most part, ignored the lesson, and went their way, like David Haggart, unrepenting.

Now it was his turn however. Three ministers, the Rev Henry Grey, the Rev Dr Anderson and Mr Porteous, the

DAVID HAGGART

Chaplain of the Jail, attended on him. Their purpose was to bring him to a proper understanding of his spiritual condition. It is hard to determine their success. On the one hand he observed the formalities of repentance. He read the Bible with which they provided him, admitted the errors of his ways, prayed dutifully, and, in his speech from the gallows eventually, 'conjured the multitude', as *The Scotsman* reported, 'to avoid the heinous crimes of disobedience to parents, inattention to the Holy Scriptures, of being idle and disorderly, and especially of Sabbath-breaking, which, he said, had led him to that shameful end'; and immediately before the hanging, after the singing of part of the twenty-third psalm, he 'knelt down and prayed fervently for a few minutes'. All that was satisfactory. On the other hand, much of his time in the condemned cell was passed in the writing of his autobiography, in which the expressions of regret are perfunctory and conventional, and the delight in his exploits real and unabated; and in the conversations with George Combe, in which he continued to promote the image of himself as a fine fellow, the very Dandy of the Sporting Life.

One attitude does not necessarily exclude the other. We have passed beyond the crude psychology that insists on absolute consistency as a test of sincerity. Instead we can recognise that contradictory emotions do not necessarily drive each other out, but can exist simultaneously in the same being, man's elasticity of temperament being such that he can accommodate such contradictions. As a lively and impressionable boy, who was, moreover, in an emotional condition heightened to an exceptional degree, David took on the colour of the moment. He did what seemed immediately appropriate; played, that is to say, the part that circumstances asked him to play.

The Scotsman reported that his conduct from the time of the trial was 'devout and penitent'. That was the proper attitude for the condemned; a certain co-operation from them being desirable if executions are to be conducted with due dignity. His father paid him a visit. The interview was 'most affecting'. David expressed satisfaction to an attendant that 'his mother was dead, as, if she had been living, his ignominious

fate would have broken her heart'. That was exactly the right
sentiment. The following day, a Tuesday, he was taken in a
chaise to the lock-up house, and, during the journey, 'he kept
his eyes intently fixed on his Bible'. On the Wednesday morning, two bailies and the three ministers accompanied him in
procession to the scaffold. 'His appearance was firm and
unshaken, and his countenance exhibited a degree of mildness
astonishing to those acquainted with the daring hardiness of
his characters and exploits. The calm serenity was changed to
an expression of grief, and he even shed a few tears on hearing
an expression of sorrow involuntarily burst from a few
women assembled in Liberton's Wynd to catch a glimpse of
his tall slender person.'

That may have been a nervous moment for the authorities
who were properly anxious that all should go off smoothly,
especially that there should be no repetition of the disgraceful
scenes that had attended Johnston's execution. However,
David quickly recovered. His behaviour on the scaffold was
henceforth all that they could wish. After singing part of
Psalm 130 – 'More than they that for morning watch my soul
waits for the Lord' – and listening to Mr Grey's 'fervent
impressive prayer, he shook hands with ministers and magistrates, bidding them farewell in a most affectionate manner'.
He then mounted two or three steps of the platform but de-
scended again to deliver his admonitory words to the people.
At last he took his station, prayed a few minutes more, gave
the signal and 'was launched into eternity'.

'He was decently dressed in black. The crowd assembled on
this occasion was immense. Everyone present appeared to be
deeply impressed with the awful exhibition. The people stood
uncovered the whole time.' With these words *The Scotsman*
ended its report of proceedings.

It had all gone off very well. David had played his part
admirably with wholly decorous complaisance, and the authorities could reflect with satisfaction that the majesty of the
law had been proclaimed, and an awful warning offered to
evil-doers. After all the justification of public executions was
just that: Voltaire, referring admittedly to a higher social
sphere, had summed it up after the execution of Admiral Byng:

43

DAVID HAGGART

'In England they shoot an admiral from time to time, to encourage the others.'

The publication of the autobiography a few days later caused some to have second thoughts. 'The publication is likely to do more harm than good', said *The Scotsman* pontifically. 'Despite the end he had come to (and despite its dignified and co-operative manner, they might have added) we fear it will rather stimulate the bad to greater exertion in crime than awaken their minds to repentance.' No doubt there was something in the complaint. Certainly the autobiography went some way to correct the impression of penitence that the execution had produced. No one could read Davy's account of his exploits without being aware of the fun and excitement he had experienced in those few years, and it is of course possible that some readers might conclude that with a little bit more luck and prudence there was no reason why so entertaining a career should be cut thus abruptly short. At the same time such admonitions as the book contained rang feebly in comparison. As *The Scotsman* put it, 'those who have done wrong frequently, and still more, those who do wrong habitually, are averse from reflection. They know it to be painful.' Accordingly the conclusion was that they were likely to let the moral of David's end pass them by, while receiving stimulation from the headlong gallop of his course.

Probably however the newspaper's fears amounted to little more than the pompous conventional platitudes in which respectability loves to garb itself. Dr Johnson provided an answer before long. In his Life of John Gay, he wrote of *The Beggar's Opera*:

'Dr Herring, afterwards Archbishop of Canterbury, censured it as giving encouragement not only to vice but to crimes by making a highwayman the hero, and dismissing him at last unpunished. It has even been said that after the exhibition of *The Beggar's Opera* the gangs of robbers were evidently multiplied. The play . . . cannot be conceived, without more speculation than life requires or admits, to be productive of much evil. Highwaymen and housebreakers seldom frequent the theatre, or mingle in any elegant diversion; nor is it possible for anyone to imagine that he may rob with safety because he sees Macheath reprieved upon the stage.'

Such robust common sense is always preferable to cant, and it is equally unlikely – whatever *The Scotsman's* apprehensions – that anyone turned to crime as a result of reading David Haggart's little book. Such productions may influence the style of criminal activity by offering the criminal a model or ideal, but the roots of crime lie deeper and are more complex. They rest in character and circumstance, and in the working of one upon the other. They are always hard to identify, and any identification can only be tentative. One thing is sure however: they are inaccessible to such glib and facile explanation.

William Bennison

Or the Other Dear Charmer

Leith Walk begins, or used to begin, in some splendour, flanked by Robert Adam's Register House on one side, and the Calton Hill on the other. Nowadays the first is deformed by the monstrous St James' Centre and the broad street is made desolate by demolition, and ridiculous by a vulgar footbridge, which could scarcely be less pleasing to the eye, and hardly even has the excuse of function.

Yet this deformity is not out of keeping with the history of the street, which has always promised more than it achieved, and this failure tells us something of the development of the city.

The street follows the line of an earthworks hurriedly thrown up in the summer of 1650 by the Covenanting Army of David Leslie to check Cromwell's advance after his victory at Dunbar. For the next century or more the earthworks stood, and were used as a walk or as a playground by children, while the road to Leith from Edinburgh continued to follow its age-old route from the Cowgate, skirting the east side of the Calton Hill and running down to the port along the lines of the present Easter Road. A curious late seventeenth-century experiment of running horse-drawn buses along Leslie's earthworks was unsuccessful, and it was not until 1774 that the decision was taken to widen and pave what became the Walk. Indeed the need to improve communications with the port was used as the common sense justification for what many considered to be the ridiculously ambitious plan to build the North Bridge over the chasm below the Old Town.

There was, it seemed, reason enough for improvement.

WILLIAM BENNISON

Leith was a busy and prosperous port. In 1791 there were five master shipbuilders there, employing one hundred and fifty two carpenters and building ships up to three hundred tons. Trade, principally with the Baltic, but also with the north German and Dutch ports, was busy. A noble street was justified.

And noble, Leith Walk certainly is – in conception at least. Wide and gently curving, it runs for a mile and a quarter down to the sea. It could have been one of the great streets of Europe, comparable for example to the Ramblas in Barcelona. Yet it is nothing of the sort, despite fine buildings still surviving at the Edinburgh end; and it never has been.

The explanation is simple and instructive. Edinburgh turned away from its port. It never developed into a great trading or industrial city. Leith has never been a focus, but at best an annexe.

This failure of development, is not immediately easy to account for. The nineteenth century saw a general turning away from the narrow seas that give on the Continent in favour of the West, the Atlantic and the Cape routes. The result was the growth of Glasgow and Liverpool, cities that grew out of their river and waterfront. Only London among eastern ports grew comparably. That was not the only reason of course: Edinburgh's industrial hinterland did not compare with Lanarkshire. There was simply nothing of the same magnitude to pass through the port. Leith's trade continued to be in timber and grain, and there was a steady East Coast carrying trade, but it was all small stuff.

As a result Leith always remained to some degrees detached from the city it served, while Edinburgh itself developed as a legal, banking and professional city. The dominance exercised by the professions has no parallel elsewhere in the United Kingdom and probably nowhere in Europe either. The 1841 Census for example recorded 7,463 Bankers, Professional Men and Capitalists out of a population of 163,726. It is safe to say that the Capitalists contributed only a small share of the total. If we give each of these four dependents – a reasonable figure considering the size of Victorian families – we find a total of almost 40,000, or something between a fifth and a quarter of the entire population of the city. And this estimate of course neglects the number of domestic servants dependent on them.

So Leith Walk never achieved the splendour implicit in its conception. The whole trend of development led away from it, as the failure of Playfair's eastern extension of the New Town also demonstrated. The proliferating middle class were rather to be found in the New Town's western extension between Charlotte Square and the Haymarket, or in the Victorian suburbs soon to be built south of the Meadows – Bruntsfield or Morningside – or to the west of Leith Walk in Inverleith and Trinity. Leith Walk itself began to decline soon after being built. By the late eighteen-sixties, when Robert Louis Stevenson was a student, its Edinburgh end was known for its taverns and brothels; it was a place you could go 'to see life'.

But the whole area became what it has never ceased to be, one favoured by immigrants. Today they are Pakistanis. Earlier this century they were Italian; before that, the Irish. The east end football club, Hibernian, with its ground at Easter Road, has an Irish name and Catholic associations; even today, though the bigotry has never reached Glaswegian proportions, supporters of the quintessentially Edinburgh Heart of Midlothian have been heard to address the Hibs as 'Fenian bastards'.

Not all Irish immigrants were Catholic however. That flood began after the Great Famine of the 1840s. Earlier arrivals were likely to be Ulster Protestants. William Bennison, bigamist and murderer, and keen member of a Wesleyan chapel, was one of those. The degree of religious enthusiasm he displayed is in fact one of the elements that makes his case and career interesting, for his crime was clumsy and mean, and his conduct crass. Yet the gap between preaching and practice, which strangely mirrors Leith Walk's failure to achieve what it promised, the existence of incompatibilities in the one character and the revelations of working-class culture which the case offers, combine to make even this story profoundly interesting.

We know nothing of Bennison's life in Ireland beyond the

fact that he married a girl called Mary Mullen. The wedding took place in Portadown in November 1838 and was celebrated in a Presbyterian kirk. There was later to be much tedious argument as to the validity of the marriage, for Bennison had been baptised a member of the Church of Ireland, which was, of course the Established Church and an Anglican community. It is hard now to feel much interest in this rather technical debate, especially since the charge of bigamy seems unimportant compared to murder. It was thought to be important in his trial, for reasons which will emerge later. Moreover the wedding suggests something of his character. Bennison combined strong sexual impulses with moral principles, or, if that is putting it rather strongly, with a powerful sense of respectability. He couldn't seduce a girl; he had to marry her.

He soon left Mary at home and came to Scotland. It was stated at his trial that he could 'assign no reason for coming here but for want of employment'; it is difficult to see why he should have been expected to do so, since this reason was obviously valid enough. Ireland before the famine was overpopulated. There is no evidence that he intended his separation from his new wife to be lasting. The plan may have been that she should follow him to Scotland when he had established himself, a common enough course in such circumstances. If so, his susceptibility soon raised an obstacle, for he had not been long in Scotland when he met and married a Paisley girl called Jean Hamilton in December 1839.

Married now to Jean, his thoughts reverted to Mary. Perhaps he saw no reason why he should not live as a sultan; there were also Biblical precedents for polygamy. Perhaps however he was simply confused. Almost certainly he did not achieve the insouciance of a Captain Macheath singing 'how happy could I be with either, were 'tother dear charmer away'. At any rate he returned to Ireland and persuaded Mary to come to Scotland with him. Perhaps she insisted on accompanying him, against his will; we have no means of telling. However that might be, his absence, according to Jean Hamilton's sister, Helen, who was to be the agent of his eventual downfall, 'caused considerable uneasiness to his wife, owing to staying away longer than the time spoken of'.

He brought Mary back and established her in Airdrie. If he intended to alternate between the two women, his determination was not put to the test, for Mary died and was buried in Airdrie in an unnamed grave. (That was probably meanness rather than duplicity, for Bennison was to show himself recurrently and unpleasantly mean.) Later there were to be suggestions that he was responsible for her death. No evidence exists to support this charge. He continued to deny it right up to the end. The least we can do is credit his word, for he had eventually motive to confess rather than to continue to deny. However, Mary's death can hardly have failed to make him realise that death can offer a satisfactory solution to matrimonial complications.

He felt constrained to wear mourning for Mary, though no one in Paisley knew of her existence, let alone her death, and he would have avoided any possible awkwardness if he had not drawn this attention on himself. Moreover, on his return to Jean, he took with him a bundle of female clothes and told his wife that the mourning was for his sister, whose clothes these were. On being asked why he had not brought her to Paisley, he replied that he had been anxious to get her to her destination, which was an old master's in Airdrie. It was as if he deliberately invited suspicion.

There was one nasty moment when he was accosted in chapel in Paisley by a little man who said,

'I think I know you.'

'Do you?'

'Was it not you that buried your wife recently in Airdrie?'

Bennison was quick to assure him that he was mistaken. He must be thinking of somebody else. The incident stuck however in Helen Glass's memory and she reported it at the trial. She also 'thought that her sister has the impression on her mind that the clothes which Bennison had brought were the clothes of another wife'.

Nevertheless Jean appeared to accept his story. Even when they visited Ireland and she met his sister, still alive, and naturally pushed her questioning further, she seemed satisfied with his new explanation that the dead girl was 'his sister in the lord'. She wasn't, likely enough, that naïve. Still Helen's version may equally well be the result of spite working on memory. One should never underestimate the human capacity for credulity, and Bennison was already so firmly in the grip of the religious enthusiasm that was to lead a witness at his trial to say that, 'his conversation was wholly confined to religious subjects', that Jean may indeed have found his explanation genuinely satisfactory. She herself was to be described as 'a very religious person'.

As to the decision to wear mourning, one can only conclude that Bennison felt a deep-seated respect for convention; it was the right thing to do and he would have been failing in his duty to himself if he had not. If this was hypocrisy, it was well-engrained.

About this time they removed to Edinburgh. For some years they lived at the bottom of Leith Walk, that natural starting point for immigrants. A daughter, named Helen after her aunt, was born in 1843. Around 1847 Bennison found work with the Shotts' Iron Company and they moved a little up the Walk to Stead's Place, a dismal row of gaunt tenements.

Their dwelling consisted of two rooms and a closet. It was on the level of the street with a sunk area below, this basement flat being inhabited by a widow, Elizabeth Wilkie. At some point in 1849 a Mrs Moffat came to live with the Bennisons, presumably as a lodger. How they were disposed is difficult to determine. Bennison and his wife slept in different rooms, Jean being evidently in the kitchen where there was probably a box bed, or rather two, for one assumes that Mrs Moffat slept there also. Across the landing was another flat, occupied by an old man, Alexander Milne, and his dog. He was to testify to the good relations between Bennison and Jean. 'I never heard angry words between him and his wife, and never heard them speak unkindly to the other.'

There was to be much argument at the trial as to the condition of the block, in particular as to whether it was infested with rats or not. The general opinion inclined to the absence of rats, at least by the time the Bennisons came to live there. Alexander Marr, one of the neighbours, certainly claimed that there had been a good many at one time, but asserted that he had smoked them out with brimstone and filled up their holes. They had come, in his opinion, from the common sewer in Leith Walk, from which there was a grating opposite Bennison's house. For good measure he added that there was another sewer at the back of the house also. Elizabeth Wilkie produced the argument that was held to settle the matter: she kept live fowls in her cellar and maintained that that would have been impossible if there had been any rats about at all. Though Alex Macmurray, a wire-worker who lived nineteen yards from the Bennisons, contradicted this, and declared that he had himself killed eleven, his dead rats had no chance in the minds of the jury against Mrs Wilkie's live fowls. The dearth of rats undoubtedly helped to hang Bennison.

Bennison worked hard at Shotts' foundry, though his habit of incessantly singing hymns and psalms failed to endear him to his fellow-workmen. He joined the local Wesleyan Church, which was not at that time considered incompatible with membership of other churches, the Wesleyans regarding themselves as a ginger-group of enthusiasts, with a consequent attraction for zealots like Bennison. It was affirmed later that he had been a lay preacher and had taught in the Sunday School. The Minister, the Rev John Hay, was quick to deny this, and to dissociate the Church from him to some degree. 'His manner was always peculiar', he said, 'he was a man excited in religious feelings.' The fact that Mr Hay's oratory had contributed to this excitement was something better ignored.

It is a minor irritation that judgements on the appearance, manner and character of murderers tend to be delivered after the event; they are therefore all too frequently governed by a *post hoc propter hoc* subjectivity. It is rare for us to have a candid picture of the murderer before he has committed his crime or stands accused of murder. Consequently he will be expected to conform to certain stereotypes: he will be 'deceptively innocent in appearance' or 'frankly sinister'. The latter was Bennison's fate. He is described as being 'of dark hair and eyes, projecting forehead, sallow complexion, very bushy whiskered.' We do not need to be told that 'his aspect is rather sinister' or directed to observe 'his prurient eye' to recognise him as a stock figure of Victorian melodrama. It naturally follows that he should be seen to fix hostile witnesses during his trial with 'an extraordinary glare'. That is casting to type, presenting a dramatically just appearance; *se non è vero, è ben trovato*. He had a strong Irish accent. It comes as a shock to discover that one of his fellow-workers complained because he was perpetually smiling.

Despite the sinister appearance that would be recognised with such certainty, no sign of villainy emerged for some years. If he had indeed murdered his first wife, he showed no mark of guilt and no desire to make a practice of it. Instead he settled into being a respectable member of the community, becoming known as a reliable worker and displaying a deep religious seriousness.

The evangelical religion to which he adhered was one of the strongest forces of the century. Essentially its appeal was emotional. It was concerned to arouse a sense of sin and personal unworthiness, so that the convert, shocked by his plight, should make a complete commitment of his soul, his being, his whole life on earth, to Christ. Evangelical meetings were rich in personal testimony, as redeemed sinner after redeemed sinner bore witness to the evil of his former ways and to the joy with which he had embraced the faith. The pastors knew that 'enthusiasm', that word which the Laodicean eighteenth century had so disdained, slackens easily; it was kept screwed to the pitch by regular prayer meetings and Bible study as well as Sunday services.

At its best – and its best was frequent – this religion aroused genuine moral fervour, and bred an insistence on high standards of behaviour. The results found full expression in the great works of Victorian philanthropy. Without the Evangelicals, attempts to bring religion to the poor and outcast would have been few indeed; practical measures to alleviate the misery of the new industrial cities equally rare. Most of what was good in nineteenth century culture will be found to have an evangelical strain.

Nevertheless there was another side. The absence of the institutional element in this religion, the lack of tradition, and the stress on personality, all combined to make it a natural home for hypocrites, exhibitionists and frauds. Confession is doubtless good for the soul, but repeated and public confession may easily become self-indulgence. Eloquence is an admirable quality, but one that corrupts when it is employed for its own sake. A consciousness of redemption is strong liquor for weak heads.

To say this is not to attribute insincerity to the enthusiasts. Only, there are always degrees and levels of sincerity, which is not a quality to be accorded an uncritical admiration; it is always fair to question the object towards which sincerity is directed. This is particularly true in the case of men like Bennison, sincere and secure in their own virtue. Yet there is no reason to suppose him a hypocrite. Hypocrisy is anyway a most wearing profession, demanding the almost permanent assumption of a mask. It is not like adultery for instance, a vice which can be practised in your spare time. The poor hypocrite can never afford to relax.

It would seem that Bennison's state was more complicated than that. His religion was genuine enough. Only, being the sort of religion that ministered to self-indulgence, a religion moreover which encouraged each devotee to be judge of his own spiritual condition, it was easily perverted to self-glorification. No one is more easily duped than the Chosen. Nothing contributes to pride like the certainty of salvation, of being one of the Elect, and the constant self-criticism which the Evangelicals, like modern Maoists, affected to practise, may fairly be regarded as an insidious form of self-flattery. 'All censure of a man's self', wrote Samuel Johnson, 'is oblique praise.' No wonder then that this intense, rambling, self-indulgent religion could breed men like Bennison who came to believe that whatever he wanted was permitted.

In the Spring of 1850 his desires became apparent. At prayer meetings he had encountered a young girl called Margaret Robertson to whom he was quickly attracted. Before long they were walking home together in the gloaming, while Bennison offered spiritual comfort and instruction, and, perhaps, other attentions that were less spiritual. For Margaret was young, pretty, devout, and, most important, admiring. Though she was later to say that she had had 'a sweetheart at the time of these meetings and it has given me pain to be supposed that I was flirting with Bennison', this putative sweetheart plays no part in the story and has never been identified. If he existed, he must, on the evidence led, have been complaisant enough. As far as Bennison was concerned, Margaret Robertson had a soul to be moulded and a body to be won. He seems to have decided in only a few weeks that she was to take the place of his wife, who (among other faults) no longer attended prayer meetings (she had a young daughter to look after) and, more to the point perhaps, did not properly appreciate him. He had fallen into the classic husband trap for weak vain men; he felt his wife did not value him sufficiently, because she esteemed him truly.

This time there could be no burying in a nameless grave, no mourning worn for a sister of the Lord. Bennison now had a certain position in the community, something he had worked for, a status that matters more acutely perhaps to the immigrant than to the native who has never felt the lack of it. Moreover, and still more pertinently, Jean had family, in particular, her sister Helen Glass now living nearby in Lochend Road, Leith. Respectability and prudence, working, as they so often do, in harness, dictated the solution. Jean had to die and her death had to be accepted as natural.

His tongue busily spread stories of her failing health. This is of course a regular device; almost the first rule of the domestic murder. There was however some evidence to back it up. Even Helen Glass admitted that Jean was 'a little delicate in winter and troubled with a cough'. Mrs Moffat, the lodger, went further: Jean 'was very weakly and much troubled with sweating'. It may have been this that had prompted Bennison to join a Funeral Society in November 1849, some months before his first recorded meeting with Margaret Robertson. There was nothing sinister in this. Such societies were the poor's only insurance. A respectable man like Bennison could not neglect such provision as would enable him to bury his wife decently, should such a sad eventuality be necessary. Yet, paradoxically, the precaution may have encouraged his mind to turn towards the course of elimination, the moment temptation appeared.

OR THE OTHER DEAR CHARMER

It is impossible to mark the moment of decision, or at least the moment of commitment. In February 1850 he went to the shop of William MacDonald, an apothecary practising in the Kirkgate, Leith, and purchased arsenic from Mrs MacDonald. MacDonald knew Bennison as 'a Christian and a pious man'. All the same Mrs MacDonald, who admitted that she never liked serving customers with arsenic, asked him why he wanted it. He replied that his wife had asked him to get it, and introduced the subject of the rats. (Sometimes one feels these stories could write themselves, so predictable are the characters' moves, as though they followed the prescribed steps of a country dance.) Mrs MacDonald warned him to be careful, and gave him the arsenic screwed up in twists of white-brown paper.

It would seem that at this point he can only just have met Margaret Robertson. One of the neighbourly witnesses, Mrs Ramsay, said that Bennison had been seen going to prayer meetings with Margaret once or twice a week for the two months before Jean's death. That would bring their meeting back to the middle of February – about the time he bought the arsenic. Others put the period of his attentions to Margaret at no more than six weeks, which would make their encounter subsequent to the purchase of the poison. It even looks as if the two might not have been connected. Yet, if they were not, the element of premeditation, which no one has doubted, begins to look unreasonable. Why should Bennison buy arsenic to get rid of his wife at that moment? Either Margaret was the spring of his motive, in which case it was simply fortunate that he already had arsenic to hand (an unlikely hypothesis), or he had met her earlier and clandestinely; or he already intended to kill Jean for some other reason. Finally, one cannot entirely exclude the possibility of innocence or of the existence of the rats.

Nothing appears to have happened till 12 April. It may be that there was a previous, unsuccessful and therefore unrecorded, attempt. It may be that he retained the arsenic in his possession for two months, brooding on his purpose. If we knew more of the movements of Mrs Moffat, the lodger, who was away on a visit to Dalkeith on the weekend of the death,

57

we might be better able to come to a satisfactory resolution of the problem. Perhaps Bennison was waiting for a weekend when she should be out of the house. On the other hand, it may be that she went to Dalkeith every weekend; there is no evidence one way or the other; merely assumptions. Nobody questioned her at the trial about her habits and movements, no significance being attached to Bennison's choice of time. Possibly of course, the arsenic had indeed been bought for the celebrated rats, employed on them, but not exhausted. It seems unlikely. Mrs Moffat declared that, 'she had never heard Mrs Bennison speak about rats, and the deceased visited the coal-cellar every night'. It would then be interesting to know what was in Bennison's mind in the two months between the purchase of the arsenic and his wife's death. Did he hope that somehow or other Jean would die, and relieve him of the responsibility of action? Could he perhaps kill her obliquely, simply by the exercise of the will? Would the Almighty take a hand and smooth his servant's path? Given his temperament, his consciousness of virtue, it seems unlikely that his hesitation was caused by uncertainty of the rights and wrongs, but he may have wondered whether he could get away with it.

There was no reason why he should not. In the nineteenth century it required no more than common prudence and tolerable competence to poison someone successfully. The celebrated practitioners like Drs Pritchard and Palmer cut swathes through their acquaintance before being discovered. What did for them in the end was lack of restraint; so many died around them that suspicion could not fail to be aroused. But for anyone less extravagant, prepared to limit himself to the essential elimination, the job was not too difficult and the prospect of discovery sufficiently remote to make the risk worth taking. No doctor's certificate of death was necessary before burial. Most of the poor died far from the reach of the medical profession. Only if doubt were already entertained were questions likely to be officially asked.

On the 9 April Bennison took another step. He joined a second Funeral society. This showed meanness and greed, quite characteristic of a certain type of murderer, and Bennison was later to display these unattractive qualities still more unpleasantly. Doubtless he saw no reason why he should pay for murdering his wife; indeed he could even make a bit on the side. The prudent man counts the pennies, and he was one of the respectable, the deserving, poor. Mrs Moffat, whose evidence of course contributed a good deal to the picture of Bennison that emerged at the trial, reported that she 'had a conversation with him about Benefit Societies, and he said that he would get £3 for the burial of his wife, besides one shilling a piece from each of the workmen; and he joined one on the ninth of the month.' Andrew Carr, secretary of the Benefit Societies, later said that Bennison would get fifty shillings from each; the equivalent of several weeks' wages, though few might think it merited a murder.

On Friday 12 April Bennison came home from his work complaining, 'and seemed rather dull', as Mrs Moffat put it. She attached no significance to his mood and set off for Dalkeith. Bennison seems to have spent the evening at home, which was by that time unusual. There was general agreement with Helen Glass's observation that 'he did not spend much of his time at home'. To explain this he had told his wife that, after working all day, 'he required exercise'; nobody had much doubt about the form this took; Euphemia Ingram, niece of neighbours called Porteous, had seen 'Margaret Robertson and Bennison walking together after it was dark'.

However there was none of that this Friday. Instead it was a quiet domestic evening. Mrs Porteous later reported that Jean had been 'in good health that day', but, according to Bennison's Declaration, she retired to bed early and then expressed a desire for porridge. Nothing unusual about that, of course, porridge not then being a dish more or less restricted to breakfast time, but the standard food of the poor throughout the day. 'They're grand food, the parritch,' as David Balfour's Uncle Ebeneezer said in *Kidnapped*.

Bennison cooked the porridge in an iron pot and then served it to her in the traditional wooden bowl. He stated that he had not been hungry himself and had therefore eaten nothing. Some porridge was left in the pot; he put it down for Sandy Marr's dog the next day. Now he settled Jean for the night and retired to bed himself.

She woke him early on the Saturday morning about seven o'clock, coming to his bedside and saying she had been unwell during the night. She had vomited several times. About an hour later she began to vomit again. There is no evidence for this account beyond Bennison's declaration, but nothing Jean said in the next forty-eight hours contradicted it.

He went to call Mrs Porteous, and asked her to come and look at his wife. She heard his story, saw Jean, and advised him to call the doctor. Bennison was loath to do so. When Mr Porteous came round and repeated the advice, Bennison told them the story of a certain Mrs O'Miggle, an acquaintance of his, who got a powder from her doctor and 'never spoke more and he did not like them'. Mr Porteous continued to advise that one be called; he remained obstinate. During the two hours that she stayed that morning she noticed that, 'whenever Bennison gave Jean anything he always stood at the crown of her head and reached forward'. It was the sort of oddity of behaviour that sticks in the mind, even though no explanation may suggest itself to account for the awkwardness.

In the afternoon the Porteous' niece, Euphemia Ingram, came in. One thing stands out clearly from the story, and that is the closeness of the community in Stead's Place. There was a constant coming and going of neighbours, who all seemed to know the Bennisons' way of life well enough too. Bennison had hardly a moment to himself the whole weekend. Perhaps he preferred it that way; it must have been a strain though. Actually his own actions contributed to this. He himself fetched Mrs Porteous, and he sent on Saturday night to acquaint Helen Glass of her sister's illness. However she was away from home, tending a sick friend, and it was not till the Sunday morning that he was able to fetch her. His behaviour may be interpreted as stupid, over-confident, innocent, or as a prudent attempt to allay suspicion.

Euphemia Ingram found Jean still retching a good deal, though there was little for her to bring up. There was some frothy water in a bowl by the bed. Euphemia saw the porridge in the iron pot and some potatoes in the kitchen. She asked if she could give the potatoes to the sow. Bennison said 'no', but she could give the porridge to Sandy's dog if she liked. This is one of the most mysterious incidents of the whole case, for the dog died the next day. If it was poisoned Bennison's stupidity passes belief. Certainly the death of the dog contributed to the suspicion that was to gather about him, even though he himself said, 'the death of the dog is nothing'. As such it might be read as one of those lapses, which would be incredible if they were not so frequent, lapses so easily avoidable that, when made, they seem to indicate a wilful dismantling of the defences that the murderer had erected with such care around his crime; so that one might almost think he desired, despite himself, to be discovered. However that might be, what is really strange about this incident is that the post-mortem examination of the dog discovered no arsenic. The dog had simply died.

Bennison also told Euphemia 'to put some dirty water into a can as there was vomiting in it, and not to empty it till night; and she did so about ten o'clock into the sewer'. Perhaps this indicates respectability and tidiness rather than guilt, though anything can be made to seem sinister when presented in evidence in a murder trial. Nor should too much be read into his peremptory manner towards Euphemia. It was natural enough that he should expect a woman to do things in the house.

Despite Jean's condition no doctor was summoned on the Saturday. That was inevitably to seem suspicious. Probably a doctor would not have saved her in any case; failure to summon medical assistance at an early moment could not itself fail to suggest that he feared the doctor's chance of success. In the declaration he emitted on 19 April he claimed that he had left the house on the Saturday about twelve o'clock in search for a doctor, but had been unsuccessful. He had gone out again about four, but did not get a doctor, as his wife would not let him.

Nobody credited this, yet it is not entirely incredible. The poor were accustomed to get their medicaments from apothecaries and even grocers – the Bennisons usually obtained theirs from a Mr Kilgour, a tea-merchant who also sold pills.

WILLIAM BENNISON

Still it would have seemed natural in the circumstances that he
should have called a doctor. After all, as early as the Saturday
morning, he told Mrs Porteous that, 'he doubted her (Jean)
very much in this bout'. His behaviour was certainly such as
to warrant suspicion. Mrs Porteous for one found him not
only strangely reluctant but secretive: she asked him if 'the
thing she had previously vomited was sour, and he answered
very drily and firmly, "no". Whenever the conversation was
about his wife,' she observed, 'he answered in the same way.'
Mrs Porteous was not favourably impressed.

Saturday night was spent by the Bennisons alone, together.
At no moment was there to be any evidence suggesting that
Mrs Bennison suspected her husband. Even when she concluded on the Sunday night that she was dying, 'she expressed
how good the Lord was to her, that she had been the weakest
vessel and was called away first'. Nothing that she said could
be construed even by hostile witnesses as an accusation. If
Bennison is to be believed on this matter, Jean was ready for
death. One of his workmates William Fairgrieve recalled a
curious conversation he had had with him. Unfortunately
Fairgrieve was unable to date it, putting it, with irritating
vagueness, 'from six to twenty-four days before her death'.
He remembered clearly enough though that Bennison had
said, 'that his wife was taken ill, and that she had advised him
to get another wife, as he would be poorly treated in lodgings'. If there was any truth in this report, Jean cannot have
been surprised by the course of events; it may even have been
this piece of advice that prompted Bennison to use the arsenic
he had already bought. One can imagine his tortuous self-
justification.

There was no improvement during the night. She weak-
ened steadily. Sunday was for Bennison a day of frenetic activity, much of which is not easy to interpret. He seems to have
decided during the night that he must now make a serious
shift to fetch some sort of medical assistance or at least get
advice. He presented himself at MacDonald's, the apothecary's, between seven and eight o'clock, and obtained powders made up of cinnamon, ginger and cayenne pepper, which
would stop the vomiting. He called Helen Glass, who had to

admit that she had got the message telling her of the illness on Saturday night, but had not then realised its seriousness. Bennison seemed to her 'much agitated'. He asked her for a little spirits, and she gave him a glass of wine. There could be no doubt that he was in a highly nervous condition.

He was now anxious also to allay the suspicions that Mr and Mrs Porteous might be entertaining. Perhaps overnight reflection had made him realise how his behaviour was likely to be interpreted. He now told them that he had been to four doctors, and they were all engaged. He named one of them, MacDonald. Porteous pointed out that MacDonald was not a doctor at all; merely a druggist.

Bennison then had the good fortune to encounter a certain Dr Gillespie, who happened to be passing his house. He urged him to come in and examine Jean. The doctor hesitated at first, 'on account', as he explained at the trial, 'of it being a dispensary case'. Presumably he was worried about his fee. This hesitation was to draw adverse comment from the Lord Justice-Clerk who inquired whether such was the normal practice of Leith doctors; things were ordered better in Edinburgh itself, where the medical profession recognised its duties towards the sick. However, having at last consented to come in, Dr Gillespie found the patient weak and vomiting. In the circumstances there was little he could do. He recommended that a mustard poultice be applied and that she be given a tablespoonful of wine every hour. One may feel that Bennison was as well off with the druggist's advice. However he pursued Gillespie to ask whether brandy would do as well as wine; he was told merely to reduce the dose.

Meanwhile, it being Sunday, news of Jean's illness was spreading. At Chapel Mr Hay offered prayers for her recovery, and when Helen Glass arrived to sit with her sister, she found Agnes Turnbull, a member of the Wesleyan congregation, already there. Agnes considered that, 'Jean's inside was in an awful state'. She watched her throw up three tablespoonfuls of vinegar and water. She sat with her into the afternoon. At some time she and Helen moved Jean from the kitchen to the bed in the other room. To Helen Jean complained of 'great pain in the stomach and bowels and of a great thirst'. Though the two powders from MacDonald had at last stopped the vomiting, it was clear that she was growing weaker.

Sometime in the afternoon Mrs Turnbull offered to fetch the doctor again, but Bennison shook his head. 'She is going home', he said. When Helen renewed the suggestion a little later, his reply was even less engaging. It would do no good, he said; so there was no need to incur this further expense. This petty callousness, this determination to save the candle-ends, is unattractive, even revolting; it reminds one of George Joseph Smith, the celebrated 'Brides-in-the-Bath' murderer, who refused to pay the instalment due on the bath in which he had drowned one of his wives, on the ground that he had no longer any use for it. Of course any notion that murder should go with an expansive temperament is romantic nonsense. A good many murders are mean, simply because their perpetrators are nasty little men. All the same Bennison's rejoinder lacks the grim, even if unconscious, humour of Smith's.

Bennison was acting in character when he refused to summon the doctor a second time. That is usually wise enough. Nothing attracts suspicion like the unusual gesture. Yet there are limits; it is equally unwise to arouse needless animosity. Husbands who appear indifferent to their dying wives are likely to displease the wife's family; and such displeasure turns easily to suspicion. Bennison would probably have been wiser to have damned the expense, and paid the second fee, even at the risk, surely an outside chance, that the doctor might still have saved her.

That was not the only evidence on Sunday that he had concluded death to be inevitable. He asked Helen and Mrs Turnbull what sort of funeral letters they thought he should get, and the following morning he took his black trousers to Mrs Ramsay, a neighbour who did tailoring repairs. Everything must be done properly. He called on the Porteouses twice, and bade them prepare for the end. It was no more than a matter of hours, he said. He was quite correct; she expired around noon on the Monday. 'I have seen many a deathbed', he told Mrs Ramsay, 'but never a pleasanter one than my wife's.' At the time he was even more ecstatic: 'Thank God she has gone to Glory,' he cried, 'she has gone home.'

Even some of his fellow enthusiasts might have considered this was overdoing it. There should be a measure in all things, and it is better that bereaved husbands show themselves at least as sensible of their own loss as of their late partner's translation to eternal bliss. Even the godly are expected to display merely human feelings on such occasions, which are rare enough to be remembered.

Of course some sort of pious sentiment was expected. Jean had already expressed herself in such terms. She was probably sincere, poor creature, as in his own peculiar way he was. Others were less easily convinced. It was not long before Helen was wondering whether the Lord had worked unaided in the affair. Almost everything Bennison did after the death might have been calculated to fan her suspicions.

He was first unduly anxious to press on with the funeral, fixing it for the Wednesday afternoon at two o'clock. Both Helen and Mr Hay were surprised by the speed. Bennison explained to the minister that, 'it did not do for poor people to keep a corpse in the house too long'. That was probably true enough, what was generally felt. No doubt in a small dwelling a corpse was not the most convenient article. There were no spare bedrooms where it could be stored. Nevertheless Bennison gave the clear impression that he wanted the body out of the way, and the whole business over and forgotten, as soon as possible.

On the same day came the death of the dog, and few were ready to believe Bennison's airy assurance that that meant nothing. At the very least it was a strange coincidence. Helen, Mrs Moffat, and Mrs Porteous all shook their heads over the matter. Tongues wagged.

Even more damning was Bennison's conduct towards Margaret Robertson. On the Monday afternoon, within a few hours of Jean's death, Mrs Porteous found Margaret making tea in the Bennisons' kitchen. She knew who she was, though she was to claim that she had never seen her in the house before. At the trial there was argument about this. Bennison stated in his declaration that Margaret had been to tea in the house before his wife's death, and even Helen had to admit, under cross-examination, that she had seen her there while her sister was alive. 'There was a bonnet sent to her to mend by her sister the week before her death, and the child went to the Robertsons' house to get a straw bonnet for her doll.' A dress-making connection scarcely justified what was happening now. Not only was Margaret there making tea, an act of enormous symbolic importance (though none of the witnesses could have described it in such words) but she and Bennison were seen together outside, walking as they had been wont to do before his wife's death. He entrusted her with the delivery of some of the invitations to the funeral, and they were seen together in the gloaming with letters in their hands – Mrs Wilkie (she of the coal-cellar fowls) stated that Miss Robertson had brought the letter inviting her son to the funeral. Worst of all, Bennison removed to the Robertsons' on the Monday evening, and spent the night there.

His behaviour defies rational explanation. It is as if he was blind to the possibility that he might be suspected of murder. He was quite remarkably stupid; stupid to the extent of imbecility, showing to a quite unusual degree, that commonly remarked criminal incapacity to associate actions with consequences. The Robertsons were equally naïve, and their complicity had never been suggested. When they realised how their reputation was compromised, their proclamations of innocence were to be loud, Margaret's sister, Mary, asserting that when Bennison visited the house, 'his conversation was always religious'. Such assurances, incapable of proof, could not of course allay scandalous rumour. The rumours were inevitable. When a man has been paying marked attention to a girl, and his wife dies, and then he moves into the girl's lodging, one cannot expect tongues to be silent.

Helen in particular wanted to know the truth. She had no special animus against Bennison. She said at the trial that she would always be grateful to him for his kindness to her sister in early years – an observation that offers a revelation of the wretched condition in which Victorian wives could languish. Helen and Bennison do not seem to have been on bad terms though. Elizabeth Grindlay, who also visited Jean on the Sunday, saw him rest his hand on Helen's shoulder at one

moment, the touch being neither evaded nor apparently re-
sented. Still, Helen did not believe the death was natural, and
she was certain her sister would not have killed herself. 'She
knew the value of her soul too well even to think of such an
act', she said. What then had happened? She made no accusation at this point. She just wanted to know. By the Tuesday
night she had a strong impression that 'something was
wrong'.

Early on the Wednesday she proposed that Jean be opened
for examination. Bennison was horrified. 'He said his feelings
could never stand it'. The subject was resumed after breakfast
and he continued obstinate. (Helen's evidence on this point
was corroborated by Mrs Moffat.) At last Bennison said that
he would bring Dr Gillespie. He disappeared for half-an-
hour, returning to say that the doctor was unavailable, being
in the country. He had then gone in search of Dr MacDonald
(as he termed him), but he was in Edinburgh attending a class.
So it was all no good.

There was nothing that could be done immediately. Bennison set off for Edinburgh himself on unspecified business.
Perhaps it was simply an excuse to be out of the house; he can
hardly be blamed for not finding its atmosphere congenial
that morning. In his absence Helen conferred with Agnes
Turnbull and another friend, Margaret Law, as well as Mrs
Moffat. They all agreed that action should be taken.

The funeral however went on as planned, there being
scarcely time to prevent it. It took place in Pilrig cemetery at
two o'clock. Bennison wore his repaired trousers, and the
deepest black. Yet even he can hardly have failed to be aware
by this time of the suspicion with which his neighbours and
acquaintance were eyeing him. Events were running out of
control. Still he had not yet lost hope of convincing Helen that
her fears were groundless, and after the funeral he called on Dr
Gillespie to tell him of the suspicions, and ask him to do what
he could to lay them to rest. Dr Gillespie, prudent man,
offered sympathy but no reassurance. The next morning Bennison was to approach Mr Hay and Mr Millar of the Ironworks to ask them to have a word with Helen. He called also
on Mr Kilgour the grocer and from him was at least able to

bring back the message that, 'Mr Kilgour was much displeased' with Helen 'for entertaining such a notion'.

If this not very convincing admonition had ever had a chance of success, it arrived too late. Helen and her friends had not been idle since the funeral. With Mrs Moffat she had spent the Wednesday afternoon discussing the case with a succession of medical men in Edinburgh. By evening they had resolved to lay information before the Fiscal. They kept this news from Bennison when they encountered him that evening (again with Margaret Robertson). He passed the Wednesday night at the Robertsons', and it was only on the Thursday morning that he learned of his sister-in-law's activities. He protested again, repeating what he had said on the Wednesday morning that 'his feelings could never stand it' and finally snapped that the exhumation should be at her expense. It was the snap of a weak man whose time was running out.

He must have considered flight. At the trial his counsel put his rejection of the idea forward as an argument of innocence. Bennison, he said, could have escaped 'seeing the great facilities that he had for doing so by railway'. It was not much of a defence, but not quite as feeble as it sounds. Liaison between police forces was still poor; crime was the concern of a locality, and, despite the circulation of descriptions and newspapers like *Hue and Cry*, it was difficult to trace a wanted man in another city. Labour, especially Irish labour, was highly mobile, and few questions were asked of a new employee. There was no national popular Press. There were no documents that would aid identification, no national insurance, tax records, no official record of existence indeed beyond that furnished by birth, marriage and death registrations; and these were often defective in cities. Consequently a quick escape by rail was possible, and a new identity in another city could be adopted without difficulty. It is easy to forget how bureaucracy and technology have restricted the freedom of the criminal.

Bennison however stayed put, but he was now agitated, alert to the danger of his position. His mind turned back to the purchase of the arsenic. If only that could somehow be wished away . . . he set off to see the MacDonalds. The conversation began obliquely. He asked Mr MacDonald if he could have a line for the medicine with which he had been supplied. The druggist assured him that was not necessary. Bennison made to leave. Then, as if the idea had just crossed his mind, he turned and asked about the arsenic. MacDonald, who knew nothing of the sale, was taken aback. Bennison explained the matter, how he had got the poison from Mrs MacDonald 'for the rats'. Since MacDonald had not been involved in the sale – Bennison suggested – surely he could truthfully deny all knowledge of the transaction? Not only Jesuits, but Wesleyans too, are capable of casuistry. Mr MacDonald however was adamant. It was as much as his position was worth; besides which it would be wrong; and what anyway had Bennison done with the stuff? Bennison replied that he had handed it over to his wife. She had mixed it in a plate, and he had never seen it since. MacDonald, though mindful of Bennison's Christian piety, was not to be persuaded. Bennison said, 'They may find it, but I declare to God that I am innocent'. It was not to be the last of his appeals to divine authority.

He returned to his house in a state of despondency. Even he could see that his position had become desperate. They would dig up his wife, find arsenic in her, and then what? All he could do was stand by the rats and proclaim innocence of anything else. It was possible that the assumption of suicide might be made . . . Mrs Moffat found him in this gloomy mood on the Thursday evening. Her own position in respect to him being at best equivocal, she can have said little to cheer him. Towards ten o'clock she made ready to leave. Perhaps she feared to compromise her reputation by spending the night alone in the house with him, but it was late enough to seek another lodging. Probably she had expected that he would betake himself to the Robertsons' again, but he was too low-spirited to act. So she decided to go elsewhere herself. She may even have been afraid. If she had, as seems probable, already concluded that Bennison was a murderer, it is natural enough that she should have felt disinclined to pass the night in his company.

Then he made an odd request. Would she please lock the

door and take the key with her? He must indeed have been in a state of abject fear and confusion. He had already given Mrs Moffat evidence of this earlier in the afternoon. Then a message had been brought asking him to call on Mr Millar, the book-keeper at the Ironworks, who was also treasurer of the two Funeral Societies. 'On coming back from the interview he fell down in a senseless state by the fireside.' She had had to revive him with a little brandy. Mr Millar had told him that in view of the uncertain circumstances of Jean's death he felt unable to pay out all the funeral money that was due. That had brought home to Bennison very starkly the nature of his position. Now he was an isolated man, and a very frightened one. He may have feared the neighbours, feared that some attack would be made on him; he may have feared that the authorities would come to arrest him, but even Bennison must have realised that they would hardly be deterred by a locked door, if they had reason to believe that he was within. Perhaps he merely wanted a night's refuge, a chance to withdraw into himself. Perhaps he spent the hours of darkness on his knees, in prayer.

If so, it failed to fortify him. When Mrs Moffat returned in the morning, he told her he had passed a miserable night. Shortly after her arrival there was a knock at the door. She opened it to find George Ferguson, a Sheriff's Officer, standing there. He had come to take Bennison into custody. It is noteworthy that suspicion was sufficiently strong to persuade the authorities to come to this decision even before the exhumation, which was in fact fixed for the next afternoon, Saturday 20 April. Bennison was still in bed when Ferguson arrived, and at first protested pathetically that he was too ill to accompany him. The objection was disregarded. He was carried off to jail.

On the Saturday morning he was brought back to the house by Ferguson and a police officer named Fallon. They took possession of the iron pot in which the porridge had been cooked, of the wooden bowl and of the tub into which Jean had vomited. They searched for evidence of rats. Both concluded that there was no way in which rats could have gained admission to the flat or even to the coal cellar. As Ferguson put it at the trial, the plaster in the cellar was 'entire'. There could be little doubt that the rats were on the run.

The exhumation was carried out that afternoon in Spring sunshine. Bennison identified the body as being that of 'my dear Jean'. It was just over a week since she had eaten the porridge, less than a week since he had summoned Dr Gillespie, and only five days since he proclaimed that 'she had gone to glory'. Now here were her mortal remains exposed again on the April afternoon, with him standing hand-cuffed beside the coffin, staring down on her face. In those few days the world had been turned upside down.

She was taken off for dissection by Dr MacLagan, and Bennison returned to jail, where he emitted the first of three declarations that he would make before his trial. In this he gave his account of the relations subsisting between him and Jean, admitting that they slept in different rooms, information that some would find sufficient cause for suspicion in itself. He then recounted his movements from the Friday evening to the Monday, stressing his many attempts to fetch medical assistance and Jean's opposition to this endeavour. He defended the innocence of his relationship with Margaret Robertson, and asserted that she had visited the house for tea before his wife's death. Finally he admitted the purchase of the poison, but stood by the story that he had handed it over to his wife to sop up the rat-holes, and had never seen it since. He was to cling to this story; there was little else he could do, and it is anyhow always hard to disprove negatives. This first declaration made no mention of his previous marriage. The second, made on 14 June, denied it, and the third of 24 June, admitted it and described the circumstances. In it he asserted that he had confessed everything to Jean 'who told him never to mention it even to her sister'. It is always convenient thus to tax the dead with responsibility.

The charge of bigamy, in itself of interest only to students concerned to disentangle the complexities of nineteenth-century marriage law, was yet to be of more general importance, for it was only the bigamy which could deprive Bennison of the reputation of a previously unblemished character. If the bigamy were to be proved, then his unscrupulousness and treachery would be clearly demonstrated; it would be shown that lust had once already corrupted the operation of his conscience, that all his piety had already proved an ineffectual barrier against the force of his animal passions, and that he was essentially unworthy of trust. Even if he were to be acquitted of the bigamy on a technicality (the defence was that members of the Church of Ireland could not contract a valid marriage celebrated according to other rites) the point would have been made by the Crown. Bennison's character would not survive the charge. Nothing else in his life, subsequent to this double marriage, showed him to be other than a good Christian and an honest man. The charge of bigamy did not establish motive, but it made the imputed motive more substantial. He had done the same sort of thing before. that is, he had permitted lust to overcome the moral scruples that should have guarded him from sin.

The trial came on in June. It was not a complicated case and required no elaborate preparation – the machinery of the law moved fast and smoothly in the mid-nineteenth century. It aroused, as any murder trial does, considerable interest. Such things were rare enough in Edinburgh. The last hanging had taken place six years before. Consequently, even though the characters and the setting of the crime were both drab, the public galleries of the court were thronged 'by highly reputable parties', as the *Evening Courant* put it.

They had defied rival attractions to attend. A Grand National Archery meeting was being held in Warrender Park and had itself attracted a field of distinguished competitors. Another draw was the Edinburgh Gymnastic Games in Belleville Park, Holyrood (the Running High Leap was won with a fine Jump of 5 ft 1 inch, and the degree of organisation may be gauged by the Evening Courant's frank admission concerning another event: 'we did not ascertain the names of the winners'.) Farther down the coast a regatta was being held at Dunbar, and all over the South of Scotland farmers delighted in the 'warm fostering weather' which was bringing on the crops after a mean spring.

Evidence for the Prosecution was led by the Solicitor-General. (In Scotland the Prosecution begins with evidence;

there is no introductory speech in which the Counsel outlines his case. This procedure is generally, and doubtless correctly, considered advantageous to the defence; the evidence is presented starkly, without the preliminary and prejudiciary gloss which an accomplished Counsel may cast on it.) The Crown's array of witnesses was long and impressive. They first dealt with the charge of bigamy, and the fact of the double marriage was clearly brought out. Whether this technically amounted to bigamy remained to be resolved; there was a case on the other side. What however was no longer in doubt was Bennison's behaviour; it had been markedly unprincipled. No jury could believe him innocent of past duplicity, hence incapable of present. His character as an honest man was gone in the first hour of the trial. Hence each piece of evidence suggesting religious zeal merely served to stamp him a hypocrite.

Helen Glass was the weightiest of the Crown's witnesses. She alone spoke with long knowledge of Bennison. She made a good impression. It was obvious that she considered Bennison guilty, and wanted him punished; but she did not make the mistake of representing him as a monster. She even paid the little tribute to his earlier behaviour towards her sister, which has already been noted. She impressed the jury as being a devoted sister, honestly and without malice disturbed by the manner of Jean's death, and therefore determined that the circumstances should be explained and the guilt brought to judgment. That was all. Nor did she yield under cross-examination. She admitted that she had heard of her sister's illness on the Saturday night, but she had been nursing a sick friend, and had not immediately realised the seriousness of Jean's condition. When she did, she came to her at once, and did not leave her bedside till death separated them. She admitted also that there had been a slight connection between Jean and Margaret Robertson, but she did not protest about this. She left the slightness – a couple of bonnets sent for mending – to speak for itself, and stand in unvarnished contrast to the number of meetings reported between Bennison and the young girl. Finally she stoutly dismissed the possibility of suicide, employing just the right religious language to convince the jury. When she left the box, the case against Bennison looked black, even though nothing had yet been said about the poison or the rats.

The evidence of the neighbours was then pieced together. Bennison's recent neglect of his wife was firmly established. His association with Margaret was made clear, its intimacy sufficiently demonstrated – the walks in the gloaming, the tea-making in his house after Jean's death, his removal to her mother's. Who could doubt that Bennison was enamoured, even if the girl was innocent and unaware of his attentions or embarrassed by them? Bennison's curious reluctance to summon medical help was brought into the open. Nobody could believe he had tried very hard to fetch a doctor on the Saturday. The story of Mrs O'Miggle shone forth in its full absurdity. Witness after witness swore the rats out of existence. MacDonald's evidence established the purchase of the arsenic, which no one still alive, other than the prisoner, had seen till Fallon, the police officer, came on some crumpled-up pieces of whitey-brown paper which had once contained the poison. The apothecary MacDonald testified to Bennison's guilty fear after the funeral, and his hopeless cry 'They may find it, but I declare to God I am innocent' rang through the courtroom. The membership of the funeral societies was made to seem sinister, as such prudence always does in such circumstances; but it took more than prudence to explain joining the second society on 9 April, a mere three days before Jean took ill. No explanation was forthcoming, and such coincidences offend rankly in the courtroom. And Bennison's dwelling, with more than one witness, on the benefits he expected, was easily made to sound mercenary. A chance remark, which the speaker himself often forgets, may be enough to hang him; words from the witness-box take on a transmuted ring.

At the core of the evidence however was the reiteration of his religious zeal, and it was this that lent the macabre tinge to what might otherwise have seemed a drab tale of a dull man, an ailing wife, and a pretty girl. Successive witnesses attested to his enthusiasm: he was 'a man excited in his religious feelings and looked happy', said Mr Hay, his pastor, showing little desire to temper the wind to this member of his flock. 'There was generally a smile on his face', he said. 'The prisoner took a great interest in the welfare of the congregation', said Joseph Kilgour the grocer. 'He brought either young or old, irrespective of parties.' 'He was a good Christian and a pious man.' So it went on, until what might have seemed evidence of moral rectitude took on a lurid hue and came rather to display the man in monstrous guise. Many in the Court and in the jury too had been brought up on the story of Major Weir, most celebrated of Edinburgh villains, who, in Stevenson's words, 'had a rare gift of supplication, and was known among admirers as Angelical Thomas. He was a tall black man, and ordinarily looked down to the ground; a grim countenance and a big nose. His garb was still a cloak, and somewhat dark, and he never went without his staff.' Except for the staff, it might almost have been a description of Bennison himself, without his diabolical smile. And the Major himself, possessed, as he ultimately claimed to be, by the Devil, had burnt with his staff for real or imagined crimes; his rare gift for impromptu prayer availing him nothing against the wiles of Satan. This dark figure was the true shadow cast by religious enthusiasm, and the horror Bennison inspired was touched with awe. The *Evening Courant* might eventually cite Bishop Lamington's work on *Enthusiasm*: 'many authors have shown a natural connection between enthusiasm and impurity', and comment on 'the apparent frequency with which the sinful appetite that led Bennison to the commission of his crime is found associated with fanatical excitement. . . .' Such sententiousness could not remove, or check, the frisson. Edinburgh was after all a city rich in places of worship. Sabbath after Sabbath, there was no movement in the streets but the steady reverent pace of worshippers. Piety and morality were to be breathed in the very air of the city. Yet here was a zealot, a man who had felt himself secure in salvation, one washed clean in the Blood of the Lamb, surrendering to carnal appetites, brought low by them, and lured finally to the comission of the most heinous act of all: the unforgivable sin of murder. It was of course a relief to reflect that he was only an Irish immigrant, living in a mean hovel at the bottom end

WILLIAM BENNISON

of Leith Walk.

It was not moral disapprobation alone that convicted him. The medical evidence was sufficiently damning. It was given by the celebrated Dr MacLagan, and it finished Bennison. From the arsenic found in Jean's stomach, tissue and liver, they had no doubt that she had taken sufficient to cause death. There was however no chemical evidence that any of the articles of food examined by them had been the vehicle for the poison. There was no evidence of arsenic in the iron pot in which the porridge had been cooked; it gave signs however of having been carefully cleaned, an action which in other circumstances might bespeak good housekeeping but in a murder trial is a clear pointer to guilt. There was evidence that the wooden tub had contained arsenic. Curiously enough there was none in the dog. Dr MacLagan then stood down, having made it absolutely clear that Jean had died of arsenic poisoning. Compared to that fact, the exact means of administration was unimportant. Unless the jury could be convinced that she had killed herself (and that verdict would fly in the face of Helen's evidence), or that she had taken the poison accidentally (which they had no reason to conclude), there was only one answer at which they could arrive. Any doubts they might have had as to the importance of establishing the method were to be swept away by the Lord Justice-Clerk in his summing-up. 'It was murder', he said, 'if an article was so placed that it was likely to be taken, even if it was not actually administered.' In effect this meant that they did not have to be certain of the means of administration in order to convict Bennison. The purchase of the poison, the establishment of motive, the record of his behaviour from the time she took ill, these were sufficient.

The defence seems to have thought so too. Mr Crawford's cross-examination of witnesses had been less than pressing; his conduct of the defence case was languid. True, he brought forward the Robertson sisters, but they seemed more anxious to save Margaret's reputation than Bennison's life. No doubt their reasoning, their instinctive reaction perhaps, was sound enough. He was doomed; she would live, and it was better she should not be tagged with the description of a murderer's whore. In this limited aim they were successful. Mr Crawford brought forward the wire-worker Alex MacMurray and his eleven dead rats, but they had too much to contend with. Finally he was reduced to the argument that Bennison would have run away if he had been guilty. He can hardly have believed it himself; certainly it failed to impress the Court. Crawford can hardly be blamed; it was an open and shut case. No wonder that he concentrated much of his attention on trying to disprove the bigamy; there was interesting legal matter there.

The Court's summing-up was unequivocal; the jury concurred. They were only out twenty minutes. Sentence was passed. Bennison was to be 'taken to the prison of Edinburgh, there to be detained and fed upon bread and water until Friday the 16th day of August and then. . . .'

If the sentence of bread and water sounds unnecessarily harsh, the reader should reflect that the mean diet was supposed to encourage penitence.

That was not Bennison's immediate frame of mind. He cried out 'in a strong Irish accent, "I am innocent before God, and I pray God this night for those who have come and stood there, declaring anything but the truth against William Bennison as he can testify from his own conscience and his own soul. I do certainly forgive them this day, and they know themselves what they have done . . ."'

So the language persists, and, in high emotion, the speaker falls back on the stereotypes of his intellectual fashion, as a means, if nothing else, of evading the realities of his situation. The last phrase is arresting. It echoes Christ's cry on the Cross: 'Father, forgive them, for they know not what they do.' Not surprisingly, Bennison could not rise to a like magnanimity: on the contrary he was sure that his enemies knew very well just what they had done.

The cry of innocence silenced the Court for a moment, as it must always do. There is something inescapably horrible in that instant in a murder trial when the accused, by now convicted, refuses to accept the verdict, but clings with vain intensity to the hope of life. They led him away still protesting innocence.

WILLIAM BENNISON

He continued to do so for the next week, sleeping badly and refusing to eat. He was not ready for death. Outside there was little public sympathy for him, and attempts to have him certified as insane met with equally sparse response. It is notable that only twenty-three out of the hundred and sixty workmates at Shotts' signed a petition asking that his sentence be commuted to life imprisonment. Meanwhile Mr Hay offered Bennison his spiritual ministrations. At last, from a mingled hope, loneliness and nostalgia for the emotional release that he knew confession would bring, Bennison gave way. He admitted it all. Everything in his religion inclined him to this course, and would probably have done so even had he been innocent. As it was, with his confession, he felt himself as one received back in the fold. Confession expunged the dreadful isolation in which he had approached despair. With confession, he could again be washed in the Blood of the Lamb. He made the best case for himself too, asserting that he had regretted giving Jean the poison almost as soon as he had administered it; certainly on the Saturday. Thenceforward he had lived in a mixture of hope and dread. This account of his emotional state was not entirely convincing. He had shown himself agitated on the Saturday and Sunday, but the complacency with which he had viwed Jean's ascension to endless bliss contradicted what he now maintained.

Nevertheless it was the best he could do. The confession was forwarded to the Home Secretary in the hope that it would procure a reprieve. Bennison began to eat and sleep, even to put on weight. He was allowed to see his daughter, and saved up some of his allowance of bread and milk for her. (It would seem that there had been some alleviation of his diet.) The interview was said to be 'affecting'. He even saw Helen Glass on whom the care of the little girl would devolve. They exchanged forgiveness. Meanwhile Bennison engaged in long sessions of prayer and Bible-reading with Mr Hay and the Prison Chaplain.

Attempts were made to persuade him to admit to having killed his first wife. He continued to deny this however. One witness did come forward claiming knowledge of the mysterious death in Airdrie, but, since he dated it two years late, it is probable that he was one of those sensation-seekers wont to concern themselves with murder cases. At any rate Bennison could not be budged. He had not murdered his first wife and that was that. Since admission would have permitted him to indulge in a new orgy of confession, it seems likely that he was telling the truth.

On the evening of Thursday 15 August he was taken in a coach from the Jail to the Lock-up House in the Royal Mile. Despite the usual precaution a crowd of sightseers spotted him. He remarked that they might have had something better to do with their time and trotted smartly from the coach to his night's lodging. Throughout the journey he had shown himself amenable and good-humoured, though a note of self-abasement readily crept in. 'Oh you may do anything you like with me, and put chains round my neck if you like', he said to the warders who were apologising for having to bind him.

Outside, a crowd began to gather before it was dark. An execution was something rare enough, and there was fun to be had even from watching the erection of the gallows. It was observed that the crowd attracted came from the poorer parts of the city and was disposed to levity. The next morning though a better social balance was to be achieved.

Bennison prayed, slept and woke to pray again. He ate a good breakfast. His mood was seen to be calm and serene, prepared to meet his Maker, in his own phrase 'to go home'. His confession had expunged his guilt – why, he had hardly been cast down by the Home Secretary's rejection of the Appeal. He thanked the jailers for their care and went forth to the scaffold in a manner that was almost jaunty.

Things were not quite so well organised there. The rarity of Edinburgh executions meant that there was no resident hangman. Accordingly they had called on Murdoch of Glasgow, an octogenarian. His undoubted experience did not fully compensate for the ravages of the years. He failed first of all to observe that Bennison was wearing a stock round his neck which obstructed the rope. Then when this was brought to his notice, he tried vainly to wrench it off. Bennison was driven to protest. 'It has a buckle' he was heard to cry. At last Murdoch managed to remove it and fix the rope. A last prayer and

WILLIAM BENNISON

William Bennison was despatched into oblivion. The *Evening Courant* remarked that, 'Murdoch discharged his revolting duties with even more of the callousness of his craft.'

That was a convenient, even soothing, criticism. At the very least it was a means of confronting the dilemma in which the act of public execution by now placed sensitive observers. Blame the hangman for its ugliness; deplore the passions of the mob; condemn the ghoulish interest; but satisfy this by a full and lucid account of proceedings. Such ambivalence is perhaps inescapable; it may be detected in the writing of this book. Murder and capital punishment are not matters on which it is easy to maintain a consistent and honest moral tone. Ambivalence may indeed be the most honest response. What is clear however from contemporary accounts of Bennison's execution is no more than what one should expect. Disquiet was growing among the more intelligent and sensitive part of the public, though the attempt to disguise it or account for it seems hypocritical. Accordingly it would not be long before executions were pushed out of sight; society might still require the death penalty as a symbol of its abhorrence of murder, or as an act of simple revenge; but it would not much longer permit revenge to be exacted in the full glare of day. Revenge would cease to be a spectacle. Instead the symbol would be veiled in the mysteries of dawn and the prison yard.

Eugene Marie Chantrelle

Or the Girl who cried Wolf

'My darling Eugene, I wish I was beside you all to-day how nice it would be. Will you write darling. Believe me my darling ever your loving Lizzie.'

'Now Eugene I want you to try and believe I love you for I do love you with all my heart I do indeed. Will you not believe that? Do believe it because I really love you. It is no fancy. I feel that I love you. I cannot forget your saying that I am heartless and unfeeling. That is not true at any rate, for I am not unfeeling. Eugene you say you will not believe what I tell you so what is the use of writing only it gives me comfort if you do not believe. Believe me my darling ever your loving

Lizzie.'

'My darling Eugene,
How could you for one moment suppose I would cease loving you. Dear Eugene I really love you I am sure as much as you love me. Did you get the note I put in your coat pocket? I am very sorry I have not been able to get beside you. I have not been out, you have no idea how well I am watched. But you know dear it is a great comfort to think you are so near me. I think you had better not walk too much in the square as people will be wondering what handsome gentleman it is walking so often. I am in an awful hurry in case of Mamma. I have only written because I could not get beside you but I will try. If your windows are to the front sit at them and I will pass on the other side or wait in the stair. Believe me my own darling Eugene ever your truly loving

Lizzie.   Burn this.'

EUGENE MARIE CHANTRELLE

Few things are less rewarding reading than the effusions of the
lovelorn and ignorant, and these naïve repetitive letters would
have neither interest nor significance but for the unhappy
sequel.

They were written by a girl of fifteen called Elizabeth
Cullen Dyer. Her character may be deduced fairly enough
from the letters, silly, unformed, her head empty except for
the conventional phrases of romantic infatuation; she was
clearly indebted to the lending library for her phraseology. At
the time of writing she was, or had recently been, a pupil at a
private academy in Newington, one of a good many similar
establishments which had sprung up to impart manners and a
veneer of accomplishment to the daughters of the bour-
geoisie. Her father was a commercial traveller for various
London houses, and the family belonged to that vast, spreading stratum of the Victorian middle class, a class which, perfectly happy with its lot and with the arrangement of society,
saw to its children's education, and lived in decent substantial
apartments (the Dyers at this time had a flat in Buccleuch
Place, a fine late eighteenth-century street, past its fashionable
peak); it was a class which took touring holidays and, most
importantly, which made a fetish of respectibility. The
wretched Elizabeth, clearly chafing under its bonds in these letters, was to be a victim on its altar. Respectability was the
great Victorian God, an idol, which demanded frequent sacri-
fice, generally, in the manner of such idols, of young maidens;
a Moloch, which took life and granted none.

The one thing unusual about these missives was their re-
cipient. Elizabeth might be indulging in calf-love, but her
adored was a mature man, Eugene Marie Chantrelle. Yet in
one sense it was not so unusual, for Chantrelle was a school-
master who had taught Lizzie French, and it is common
enough for immature girls to develop a passionate devotion
for their instructors. Moreover, since early photographs of
Lizzie show a soft and dewy prettiness, it is not in turn surprising that she aroused Chantrelle's desire.

Chantrelle had been born in Nantes in 1834. His father,
who was a shipowner in that prosperous Breton port, gave his

son a good education, which included a course of study at Nantes Medical School. He was later to pursue further medical studies in Strasbourg and Paris, and, for one year, much later, in Edinburgh. He called himself a medical man, and was accustomed to dispense prescriptions for family, friends and acquaintances, though he had never acquired a medical degree. However, by his own account, he could have done so at any time, 'having studied medicine in the highest degree' – Chantrelle gave most people he met the impression that he did not think too badly of himself and his own capabilities.

The history of his early career is confused, more than one account having been given at different times. According to one version, he left France in consequence of Louis Napoleon's coup in December 1851, but he also claimed to have studied medicine at Strasbourg from 1850 to 1855. Whatever the truth, and one claim must exclude the other, he certainly found it convenient and agreeable to his consequence to present himself as a political refugee. He would say he had fought on the barricades, and would then display an old sabre wound in his arm; in the right quarters – those that would admire and those that would be shocked – he would admit to having formed strong communist opinions in his youth. He travelled for some years in the United States, without ever establishing himself there; and it may be held that a man who could not achieve that in the middle of the nineteenth century was flawed in some important respect. The early 1860's saw him established in England, in Newcastle and then in Leicester and other places, where he found employment as a teacher of his native language. In the middle of the decade he removed to Edinburgh, where, after another flirtation with medical training, he set up as a teacher of French, Latin and Greek. Though he continued, as we have seen, to describe himself as a medical man, and was always ready to prescribe for those, who, for one reason or another, wished to have nothing to do with the regular doctors, his principal energies were now devoted to instruction. He met with a good deal of immediate success. He was after all a man of the world with at least a veneer of superior culture. His manners were polished, and he enhanced his reputation by producing textbooks, sufficiently well made

83

to be used in many schools. By the year 1867 when he met Elizabeth Dyer, he could consider that, after many vagaries, he had found a position which offered him a certain stability and standing.

These vagaries had been real enough, sufficiently serious to endanger any hopes of a respectable career. There were certainly things to be kept hidden from Lizzie and her mother. *The Scotsman's* obituary was to record that while acting as tutor 'in various families of the highest respectability in England, Chantrelle committed what, so far as is known, was the first outrage that brought him into the hands of the police – an outrage of a very gross nature, which would, it is believed, have been followed with penal servitude, had it not been for the high testimony to his character borne by the family with whom he had resided, and which, as it was, brought about a sentence of nine months' imprisonment.' Moreover, 'in 1866 soon after this term of confinement was over, he came to Edinburgh, where he was guilty of an act which was nothing less than a shocking repetition of his former offence. For this heartless crime no steps were taken against him.' The newspaper assigns no reason for such leniency; one can only assume a desire to protect his partner in this disgraceful occurrence, a partner who was probably a minor. Thus early in his carrer did respectability help to shield vice and crime.

Lizzie was not the only girl he is known to have seduced. There was another, a governess called Lucy Holmes, seduced in his lodging one New Year's Day, and then abandoned. She wrote pathetically to him from Cromer that summer:

'. . . What happened in your house on the 1st of January, and how you shielded my fears, by assuring me that nothing would result from what you had done, which I in my simplicity fully believed, but now I find that you have been deceiving me all the time, if not yourself as well. Think for a moment what you would feel were your only sister to be treated as you have treated me . . .'

The appeal was vain. Chantrelle, not surprisingly, was

proof against such pathos, unmoved by the thought of what his emotions might have been had his putative sister been similarly abused; he could bear such reflections with the most stoical equanimity.

Yet, even if such rumours surrounded him, they only added to his attractions. There can be no doubt he was an object of glamour to the girls he taught. A photograph taken in 1867 shows a well set-up man, with a straight nose, high forehead, brown and gently waving hair. The great Dundreary whiskers cannot quite disguise a suggestion of humour. He looks the very model of a Victorian hero, a maiden's dream, and it is likely that Elizabeth Dyer was not the only girl at school to think so. It was equally unsurprising that her parents did not share her enthusiasm, or even like the association. Their reasons were clear enough. Chantrelle was a foreigner. He was, at thirty-four, just twice Elizabeth's age. They knew nothing of his family, and nothing of his early life, beyond what he condescended to impart. Very probably they found it hard to know how much of this they should believe, for Chantrelle had no low opinion of his capacity, was inclined therefore to be a braggart, and was extremely vague as to dates, and cavalier in his regard of fact. He was to state, in his first Declaration to the magistrates, for instance that, 'I was married to my late wife on 2nd August, 1868. I had made her acquaintance about eighteen months previously. She was then a pupil of mine at Mr McLachlan's school in Arniston Place. She was then fourteen or fifteen years of age. She was sixteen when we were married, but I forget when her birthday was . . .'

But he went on immediately to say, 'no attachment was formed between us until I became aquainted with her family, which was eighteen months or two years after I became acquainted with herself . . .' and then, 'I knew my wife as my pupil for about two years before our marriage and also for about a year during which I courted her after she left school – our acquaintance before marriage being in all about three years.'

All that was confusing enough, especially as there is no evidence that Chantrelle was teaching in Edinburgh as early as

EUGENE MARIE CHANTRELLE

1865. (Mrs Dyer by the way put the date of the wedding as 11, not 2 August.)

Whatever her family's doubts, Elizabeth was besotted with Chantrelle. She made as much of the running as he did, and she was only too ready to throw herself at his feet:

> 'Oh Eugene you do not know how I love you. I could never bear anyone to kiss and pet me. If it was broken off I should die. You think perhaps I do not mean it but really I could not live without your love. . . .' . . . 'I feel my love increasing daily as I am never content but with you . . . you do not know how intensely I love you far more than I did . . . I want you to ask them to let me come to school for French as we will be out together walking. How different it will be when we are married we shall have no one to bother us . . . I wish I had you here, but as it is impossible at present I send you kisses without number. . . .'

It is hard, as in all such cases, to determine how far Elizabeth was merely responding to her notion of what a young girl should write to her lover – the stereotype of passion is evidently there. All the same one cannot fail a detect a note of sincerity sounding through the stock phrases and self-dramatisation. Lizzie was certainly fixed on her prey.

The affair went the full cycle of devotion, renunciation, outbursts of jealousy (mostly on Chantrelle's part), recriminations and reconciliation. They both played it as Grand Opera. As early as October 1867, for instance, ten months before marriage, Lizzie could write: 'My Darling Eugene, as it would make me very unhappy should our arrangement be continued I therefore release you from all your engagements to me. . . .'

And he would reply in the full flow of melodrama: 'My house is always open to you whenever you choose to come, but I will NEVER enter yours again . . .'

How different, she must have felt, from the timid passions and staid boyish emotions of her friends' respectable and clerkly suitors. Yet, at the same time and in the right place, Eugene could show tenderness enough: 'Why do you want to die, you foolish little puss; there are many happy days in store for you yet. . . .'

The affair had to come to a point, and, whether by design or not, there was one sure way of bringing it there: Lizzie became pregnant. This gave her the opportunity for a splurge of emotion, fully revealing both of her confusion and of her fidelity to the part written for her.

'My darling Eugene,

I scarcely know how I managed to pass last night. I try to think that you are right and know better than me, but still I expected you would come. Never mind what Papa says. I know that they wanted to get you a carpet for the bedroom because they were going to give us a bed and wardrobe which is bought. But I don't see what more is wanted. But what is the use of speaking about what is not to be. The only thing I can do is to go away as it is evident I cannot stay and have a baby at home. . . .'

It is quite true what Mamma says that when you give yourself to a man he loses all respect for you. But I do not say so of you Eugene . . .' (One may ask, what then is she saying? How stands Mamma's conventional wisdom about loss of respect?) . . . 'I do not complain the thing is done and I am ruined for life. The only thing for me is to go to the street and shorten my life. I never thought, but it is useless speaking. . . .'

And she ends by saying that she will get her brother John to call on Chantrelle on his way home – 'it will be the last time I will ever trouble you. . . .'

But of course it wasn't. Now, while it would be cruel and invidious to question the sincerity and the note of despair in this letter, it is hard not to read it also as the work of a poseuse; Lizzie cannot wholly hide her enjoyment of her plight. She had found herself bang in the middle of a stock melodrama, and had no doubt whatsoever of how her part should be played.

The next step was a secret marriage. On 10 May, in Chantrelle's rooms in George Street, Eugene and Lizzie plighted their troth, exchanging notes in which they accepted each other as husband and wife; a sufficient ceremony to make them legally wed according to Scots Law. By August they had prevailed, and were publicly married. Her parents did not like it – how should they? – but, with their daughter seven months pregnant, opposition was pointless; it was a question simply of avoiding disgrace. Relations between mother and daughter never wholly recovered. 'I visited my daughter occasionally throughout the period of her married life, and she and the children called on me sometimes, but not as frequently as I visited them', she was to testify in a tone of undisguised frostiness. Lizzie had come near to disgracing them once, had indeed to some extent done so, for it cannot be imagined that Mrs Dyer did not lose face because of the short interval between her daughter's marriage and the birth of her first grandchild. Accordingly it was to be an article of the first order with the family that Lizzie should be prevented from any course of action that would incur further odious publicity. This stony-faced attitude contributed to intermittent misery, and probably to her death.

The marriage was turbulent from the start, and, on the face of it, unhappy. The qualification is necessary, for enough evidence as to the characters of both Chantrelle and Lizzie exists to suggest that both liked to live in an atmosphere of high drama; and that the turbulence kept boredom at bay, and might indeed be said to be their natural element. This is something that should be borne in mind. Neither was fit for a calm. They could exist in an atmosphere that would reduce others to despair. We should not therefore be overquick to assume Lizzie's misery. The marriage was always exciting; both were actors; and there is some evidence that a degree of tenderness and affection persisted, even if it was only displayed or experienced from time to time.

Difficulties were obvious straightaway, and they were not all felt by Lizzie. Chantrelle after all had probably not bargained on marriage. It was something he had been forced into. In a sense Lizzie had outwitted him. With even the best will in the world – and that was lacking – it is difficult for a bachelor in his middle thirties to adapt to marriage with a seventeen year old girl. He was – there can be no doubt about it – paying for his little bit of fun. For three years before his marriage, he had shared his apartment with a young man called Driggs, who may have been an ex-pupil. In time Driggs' family, mother and sisters, came to lodge there too. Not unnaturally Lizzie objected to this arrangement. She made scenes and the Driggses were successfully expelled. This victory of Lizzie's was expensive for her husband, who now had to defray the growing costs of the whole establishment. There is no reason to suppose that he experienced a corresponding or compensatory increase in his income; he maintained indeed that the Driggses were worth £250 a year to him. Throughout the ten years of his married life, Chantrelle was dogged by financial worries, thickening as the years passed, until at last he reached a point of desperation. Only those who have never experienced them can be blind to the demoralising effects of debt and pecuniary embarrassment. Chantrelle did not react intelligently or admirably to these difficulties, but the tenor of his behaviour is not hard to understand, and was by no means unusual.

They lived throughout their married life in George Street, a central but hardly fashionable address, other areas of the New Town, and the spreading suburbs of Morningside, Grange and Inverleith being more in demand. Their accommodation was adequate but hardly spacious, a double flat occupying the top two floors of 81a. It consisted of a kitchen, dining room, parlour and classroom (for Chantrelle gave some lessons at home) on the lower floor, and two bedrooms in the attic. Since there were eventually three children as well as a resident maid, the accommodation was only just sufficient. (The maid slept in the kitchen, or in an annexe to it, though at times she slept across the bottom of Lizzie's bed.) By 1877 Chantrelle and his wife no longer shared a bedroom, he sleeping in the front room, also called the nursery, with the two boys Eugene (also known as Jack) and Louis.

Chantrelle was not by temperament a family man, though he was fond of the children. He was not much in the house, except when teaching, and took few of his meals with the family. He usually taught at home from nine to ten in the morning, and again sometimes in the evening from seven to nine-thirty. He had another pupil who came some afternoons from two to three, and two young ladies who came on Saturday mornings from twelve to one. Since he also taught at Leith High School, and perhaps privately at other addresses, he had, even at the end, (for these times were given by Mary Byrne, the maid with them in the last year) a sufficiently full teaching load. He can hardly be accused of not working to support his family. Yet Lizzie complained that his teaching was falling off.

That could have been true, for his habits had become increasingly dissipated. By the mid seventies he was certainly drinking excessively. The maid computed that he would get through a bottle of whisky a day, and added that she had also seen him drink wine. Since he regularly had a glass of whisky brought up with his early morning cup of tea, there can be little doubt that he had come to depend on alcohol. (The maid's estimate ignores anything that he drank out of the house, of course, and he was a regular habitue of the local hotels. On New Year's Day 1878, for instance, the day Lizzie took ill, he spent the afternoon in the Hanover Hotel round the corner from one o'clock till a quarter past four.) There is indeed good reason to suppose that he had drifted into the dangerous, though not hopeless, condition of the man who relies on alcohol to keep him going, who can hardly conceive life without it, and who does not observe how his faculties are distorted, and his moral judgement impaired, by the very drug on which he depends.

Drink wasn't his only dissipation. He was well known as a frequenter of the brothels situated in Clyde Street, a narrow insalubrious lane to the north of George Street. In 1876 when Lizzie approached a private detective with the request that he report on her husband's movements, she was assured that that was hardly necessary, as the detective himself had seen him in a brothel. At Chantrelle's trial the Crown called one Barbara Kay, who proudly described herself as the keeper of a brothel, but her evidence was dispensed with, the point being already accepted. Later, legends were to grow about this. Sir Henry Littlejohn, Surgeon of Police, told the criminologist W.N.

Roughead, that it was Chantrelle's practice to take a loaded pistol with him to the brothels, 'which he would playfully discharge to the terror of his entertainers'. Presumably only a good customer could get away with such conduct. No doubt there was a good deal of unsavoury evidence, as was shown by the Defence's readiness to accept the fact and skate over its implications as quickly as possible. Chantrelle's Counsel was to try to excuse his conduct in this, and other respects, in which he fell short of the standards to be expected from a father of a family, by reminding the jury of Chantrelle's nationality. It was not to be expected that a Frenchman would behave as morally as a Scot.

Worse even than this immorality was his violence. Some of it was certainly no more than violence of language – ex-servant after ex-servant reported that he called his wife frightful names, many of them too awful to bear repetition. The least offensive were 'bitch' and 'whore'. He did not however always stop at words. Not only did he frequently threaten to kill her (with poison, in the use of which he boasted of his ability to outsmart the professors), but he struck her on a number of occasions. Such rows were common in the early years of their marriage, a holiday at Portobello in 1871 being particularly memorable . . . Lizzie wrote to her mother:

'I might have been sleeping for an hour or more when I was awakened by several severe blows. I got one on the side of my head which knocked me stupid. When I came to myself I could not move my face, and this morning I find my jaw bone out of its place my mouth inside skinned and festering and my face all swollen. The servants who sleep in the next room heard it all, besides the woman to whom the house belongs. They heard him say that he would make *mincemeat* of me . . . well mamma if you do not want me to be murdered outright you must see that all I can do is leave him at once. All I hope is that he may go away too. As to getting anything from him impossible. But surely where life is concerned you would never hesitate . . . I am sorry to trouble you but if he murders me you might have been sorry not to have heard from me. . . .'

EUGENE MARIE CHANTRELLE

An ingenuous and surely unexceptional conclusion.

Her next letter repeated that, 'the threats are something fearful' but, oddly, went on at once to complain that, 'it is very dull here'. That letter was intercepted by her uncle James Cullen, who sent it on to the girl's mother with a scribbled postscript saying, 'I opened it in case of urgency'. Clearly however he found nothing urgent in the frightful threats. A few days later Lizzie wrote again, this time to recount a scene so alarming that the maids had gone out in search of a police-man. They had returned with two officers, but Lizzie had per-suaded them to go away. 'I should not have been afraid of three, but he could have fought the two easily', a curious reason, especially as she went on to say, 'Christina heard him say that he would murder me and the children'.

None of these pictures of life chez Chantrelle roused Mrs Dyer to action. Possibly she was indifferent to her daughter's fate; possibly she was averse to the scandal that a separation would attract; most probably she was fully aware of Lizzie's love of self-dramatisation. Chantrelle himself was to stress this element in her character in his first declaration to the magistrates on 8 January, 1878:

> 'There was a great deal of affection between my late wife and myself, but she was sometimes funny; for instance, when I was going out to teach at Leith High School she would tell me she was going to drown herself. This hap-pened several times, and I would say "Nonsense, my dear, what would you do that for?" One Saturday, when she played the same game, I was so annoyed that I said to her, "Go ahead and do it."'

She did not obey, and it seems likely that Mrs Dyer received her fears of being murdered with something of the same scept-icism. That did not mean that she abated her dislike and distrust of her son-in-law; merely that she chose not to be over-concerned by fears that she thought exaggerated and, in a sense, self-indulgent. All the same, on several occasions during her marriage, Lizzie did run away from her husband

and take refuge with her mother. But the breach never lasted long. For one thing, as Chantrelle maintained, 'she could not be there long without a big fight'.

Although these fears might be exaggerated, they were not wholly vain. Independent evidence of Chantrelle's violence exists. Two servants saw Lizzie struck and Chantrelle was certainly fond of brandishing his pistols, which he kept loaded. (He liked to fire at the parlour or schoolroom wall, also.) On their last summer holiday at Portobello in August 1877, there was an accident involving their eldest child, Eugene, an accident that was to take on a gloomy significance. Moreover, the previous year, Chantrelle's behaviour to Lizzie and their servant once became so alarming that the two women sallied out into George Street in the middle of the night to fetch a policeman. Sergeant Robert Brass recounted the incident in the following terms:

'On Sunday, 30th April, 1876, when I was in Hanover Street, Madame Chantrelle and a servant came up to me about 4.30 in the morning. They were not fully dressed. Madame told me that her husband had come in and broken into the servant's bedroom, and threatened herself. He threatened to use violence to her.'

Asked whether Lizzie had said anything about her husband's treatment of her in general, Sergeant Brass replied, 'That it was very cruel. She said she could not put up with it any longer, and that I must take him to the Police Office. She said he had struck her repeatedly and that the language he used to her was very bad and of an obscene kind. She said, also, that his habits were very bad, and that he went about the nighthouses, and that, if he was taken to the Police Office, her friends might take up the case and get a separation for her . . . When I went to the house the door was opened by the Prisoner. I think he had been drinking. I apprehended him. When I told him that he must come with me to the Police Office he lifted a butter-knife that was on the table. He used obscene language. He threatened his wife more than once then, and on the way to the Police Office he said, "I will do for the bitch

93

yet" . . . He was convicted in the Police Court and bound over to keep the peace.'

It had been an awkward and ugly scene, even if not without its ridiculous aspects, the butter-knife, for instance, hardly being the most terrible of weapons. To another policeman, Constable McKenzie, who interviewed Lizzie the following day, the poor girl expatiated on the incident. She told him, 'that her husband was very drunk on the Saturday night and Sunday morning, and that when the servant went into the room to see that the gas was all right, he threatened to strike her. Madame Chantrelle went into the room to save the servant and he threatened to do the same to her if she interfered. . . . She was very much afraid of his ill-usage when he returned home at night under the influence of drink.'

The last is the crucial phrase. There can be little doubt that drink contributed to Chantrelle's violence, releasing the pent-up resentment of a man who felt that somehow life had cheated him; that its rewards were less than his talents deserved. Yet this realisation sets the marriage in better perspective – it was unsatisfactory but a good deal less than absolutely intolerable. Since Chantrelle continued able to fulfil his teaching duties, it is likely that the drunkenness and accompanying violence were intermittent. Certainly he maintained a good reputation in some quarters. When he applied for the vacant post of French master at the High School in 1877 he was able to support his application with no fewer than nineteen testimonials from prominent citizens. That he did not succeed in obtaining the position does not prove anything against him; there may simply have been a more obviously suitable candidate. Of course in a city like Edinburgh there were inevitably rumours suggesting that he was not perhaps the most entirely appropriate instructor of the young; even in a school where there were no girls.

Causes for quarrels were not hard to seek. Both Chantrelle and Lizzie were jealous. In his Declaration he stated that she was 'extremely' so. 'She would object to my taking my hat off to a pupil, and to all sorts of things. On one occasion I was smoking and sipping my coffee after dinner when she came into the room and looked daggers at me and walked away. She afterwards asked me what I meant looking at "that woman". I assumed she meant a woman whom I saw at a lodging-house window opposite. She said, "what do you mean by stroking your chin at her?" I told her that I never did this at a woman in my life.' Lizzie of course had lively reason for her suspicions. She knew from her own experience before marriage that Chantrelle was not likely to allow his desire to be controlled by morality or even prudence. (He of course knew the same was true of her.) She was also aware that he regularly made advances to their servants, and she was quick to accuse him of this, even when evidence was lacking.

One such accusation, according to Chantrelle, rebounded on her. This servant, whose name he could not remember – 'I never do recall the names of servants who have been with us' – was dismissed by Lizzie on mere suspicion. She returned the next day, supported by her aunt, whose presence she hoped would lend authority to her narrative, to inform Chantrelle that his wife had been carrying on an intrigue with a young man who lived on the common stair. Chantrelle investigated the matter, and, though unable to prove anything beyond the fact that Lizzie and the young man had chatted together, yet contrived to extract an apology from him.

Of course Chantrelle was jealous – he had a high sense of what was due to him. Moreover he knew Lizzie was beautiful and desirable – had not he desired her himself? He knew she was susceptible; had he not seduced her? He could hardly believe her chaste, nor could he believe that her virtue had grown with experience. He soon detected another liaison. The same servant-girl was his informant. Through her he discovered that a certain young man, who worked in a bank, had given Lizzie a scent bottle, while she had given him a cigar case in return. Incensed by this exchange of presents, Chantrelle set to work. He obtained a cigar case of the same pattern from the same shop, confirming, as he did so, that Lizzie had made a purchase the previous Christmas. After a number of accusations, which elicited only violent denials from Lizzie, Chantrelle confronted her with the cigar case. 'She took a good deal of persuadion, and at length confessed to repeated adulterous intercourse', he declared. Again he obtained an apology, and this time also a *solatium* of £50, which he claimed to have sent to the hospital in Nantes by way of his aunt.

These were the only two affairs he claimed to have detected, and though there is undeniably something offensive in his pose as an injured party, there is nothing incredible in his accusations. Given the character and the circumstances of the marriage, they seem probable enough. Moreover, contemporary *mores* may be held to some extent to mitigate the offensiveness of Chantrelle's behaviour. One law for men and another for women was, in the nineteenth century, a given truth, almost unchallenged.

However, Chantrelle did make one other accusation, so gross and scandalous that he did not dare to repeat it in his Declaration; possibly because he could bring nothing to substantiate it. This was a charge of incest. Lizzie had a twin brother, John, to whom she was close, though no more so than twins often are. Chantrelle chose to find something excessive in their relationship. In August 1874 he wrote to John Dyer in the following extraordinary terms.

'Sir,

I find that on the 21st ulto, you were in my house for a considerable time, and remained with my wife alone, my elder boy Eugene being carefully kept out of the way on some futile pretext, and not allowed to come in during the time you were there.

My wife, your own sister, having refused at first, denied that you were in the house at all, and having afterwards refused to answer any questions about the way in which you spent your time together, I beg of you to give me full information as to: 1st how and for what purpose you came to be invited to my house in my absence. 2ndly How and in what manner you spent the considerable time that you were there.

I wish to make no insinuations of any kind for the present, what I object to in the meantime, is the mysterious way in which the meeting of you and my wife took place, and the amount of untruths which she has told me with regard to this business, namely giving me deliberately and wilfully, I suppose, the wrong address, when I wished to call on you to have a personal interview.

I shall wait until 12 o'clock p.m., Tuesday the 4th inst, for your answer, which must be categorical, and clear, and full. Failing which, I shall see what further steps to take.

Believe me, I wish to keep this matter between us, if possible; this will depend entirely on you.

> Your obedly,
> E Chantrelle.'

This was the letter of a man whose balance was at best precarious, whose propensity to suspicion and jealousy was extreme. Yet, taken as we have it in isolation, it may be misleading; that is, not knowing what had preceded it, we may fail to interpret it properly. It is possible that Chantrelle's suspicions were not entirely absurd; or that there had been some earlier occurrence which had led him to try to impose a ban on his brother-in-law. The first interpretation, that it displays a morbid jealousy, is doubtless more probable; the alternative should not be dismissed as unthinkable. Certainly, this letter, and the accounts of the young man on the stair and the other in the bank, go to suggest that Chantrelle never became indifferent to his wife.

In fact, such evidence as there is indicates that relations between them showed some improvement in the last eighteen months of her life. It was as if the Police Court incident had helped to pull him up. It had had an effect on Lizzie too. Her immediate reaction had been that she had had enough. She must get away from this man. Accordingly she had allowed the private detective McDonald (who had told her that he had seen her husband in the brothels) to take her to a solicitor called Charles Hogg. She told Mr Hogg that she wanted a separation from her husband, and assured him, 'that there would be no difficulty in getting evidence of adultery and of frequenting brothels'; there, after all, was Mr McDonald to offer it. However, she then came to the heart of the matter; would there be, 'any exposure about it'? Mr Hogg had to admit that it was probable there would be some. That was enough. Lizzie shook her head and stated that, 'on that

97

ground, for the sake of her friends and family, she would not proceed'.

It had been at best a half-hearted attempt. Her hesitation was natural. She was afraid of losing the children, and, without the assurance of support from her own family, dared not proceed. Possibly her feelings about Chantrelle were still mixed. The most cogent argument was social. As a married woman she had a respectable position, whatever the circumstances of her married life. Separated, her situation would be quite changed. It was not a course she dared embark on without encouragement. Moreover, according to Mrs Dyer, Chantrelle had threatened Lizzie that he would shoot her if she left him. Unfortunately Mrs Dyer could not recall the date of that particular threat, any more than she could remember just when he had said he would blow up her house if Lizzie went to live there. None of this had been enough for Mrs Dyer, who had never gone so far as to consult a professional man about her daughter's rights, 'to have the children if she was separated from her husband when he was ill-treating her'. One cannot escape the conclusion that Mrs Dyer preferred that her daughter should endure suffering so that she might remain respectable. That is, if she believed what Lizzie told her in the first place.

So Lizzie stayed, and matters went a little easier. True, Mary Byrne, their last servant, did not find much to commend in Chantrelle's behaviour to his wife: 'he was not very kind to her. He never went out with her; he was not very attentive ... they did not get on very well together ... he used bad language to her ... I heard him say to her "Go to hell" and "Go to stay with your mother". .... On the other hand she could not 'recollect any strong language in George Street after coming up from Portobello'; and she admitted that Christmas 1877 had passed off pleasantly: 'Master, mistress and children dined together that day. There was something extra on that day – a pudding and a bottle of champagne. So far as I could see, the family were happy and spent a merry Christmas.'

She was supported in this by the most pathetic evidence offered at the trial, that of the Chantrelles' oldest child, young

Eugene. The boy admitted that he had seen his father strike his mother, and heard him call her bad names, but, after testifying to his father's invariable kindness and generosity towards himself and his brothers, said, 'he was kind to Mamma too. It was a long time before Mamma died that the hard words and the swearing took place. I can't say how long since he struck her on the head. It was in George Street before we went to Portobello. Papa was kind to Mamma lately. I had nothing to cry for for a good while before Mamma died. We all dined together on Christmas Day. We had a bottle of champagne, and papa and mamma were kind to each other. There was no quarrelling nor were there bad words. . . .'

Such evidence rang with the truthful innocence of pathos, but could still be made to sound sinister. When a couple who have been on notoriously bad terms are then reconciled for no apparent reason, and this reconciliation is soon followed by the death of one of the parties, the experienced reader of detective fiction has no doubt whom the police will first suspect. In a sense, of course, the accused in a murder trial is in a hopeless position, when the circumstances are like this. If he continues on bad terms with his spouse, that is evidence of motive; if he effects a reconciliation, that is mere duplicity, and the motive remains there, working under the surface. Motive never evaporates.

The jury were not to be impressed by this evidence of improved relations. Other aspects of Chantrelle's condition and circumstances in the autumn of 1877 were calculated to carry more weight with them. First, there was the evidence of his continued heavy drinking and consequent neglect of Lizzie. Mary Byrne's account of his alcoholic habits was full and convincing. 'He took a good deal to drink. He took whisky and water. He finished about a bottle a day. It was shortly after we came up from Portobello that I noticed he was taking that large amount of liquor. I could notice the effects on him.' The jury would have little doubt what conclusions to draw from that sort of evidence.

Even more impressive was what they were to learn of Chantrelle's financial difficulties; these were the real thing, proof positive that he could not be trusted, for he had offended the first law of Victorian wisdom: 'whom the Gods love, die rich'. The Lord Advocate summed up the position with succinct distaste in his address to the jury:

> 'He was not a penniless man; but he was a needy man. He was asking till Christmas time to pay a small balance of a bill for £18. The balance at his banker's had disappeared. His wife told Mrs Baird that her husband's teaching was falling off, and that they would probably have to go to London; and she told her mother that they were £200 in debt and had nothing to pay it with.'

This was not quite accurate – it was her brother she told, not her mother; but the impression conveyed of a man desperately searching for money was supported by other evidence, and nowhere contradicted. True, there was no evidence beyond that offered by Mrs Baird, an old friend of Lizzie's now settled in London, as to the decline in Chantrelle's business, and it might seem to be contradicted by Mary Byrne's account of his teaching hours. Still, it is, for reasons already adumbrated, likely enough that he was less in demand, partly perhaps from a growing disinclination on his part, this disinclination being fostered by his developing alcoholism. He had been teaching for a good many years; it would not be surprising if he was bored and disillusioned, especially since his particular branch of teaching is one which makes heavy demands on the instructor's enthusiasm and persistence; both qualities which alcoholic addiction will dull.

Certainly that autumn he was looking for an alternative source of income. In September the Scottish manager of the Star Accidental Assurance Company advertised for agents. Chantrelle applied. He was appointed on the basis of his written application, without references being taken up. Yet, if he intended to make something of this, he lacked the necessary perseverance. He only did one bit of business for the Company, persuading an acquaintance, one William Reid, an upholsterer in George Street to whom Chantrelle had acted as medical adviser, to insure against accidental death. His only other contact with the Company was curious, and considerable emphasis was laid on it at the trial.

This was a conversation he had with Mr Macwhinnie, the manager, as to just what constituted an accident under an accidental insurance policy. He began by saying that he had recently met with an accident himself, which had turned his thoughts to the subject. (It was true; he referred to the occasion at Portobello, when young Eugene had inadvertently fired one of Chantrelle's pistols, lodging a ball in his father's thumb.) Chantrelle now told Macwhinnie of a friend who had died, in mysterious circumstances, after eating a Welsh Rarebit, Macwhinnie was certain that such a death would not be covered by the policy, even though the doctors had not been able to say what he had died of. There would have to be an ascertained cause of death. Chantrelle then brought up the case of a person who went out swimming, say at Portobello, caught cramp and drowned; how about that? Would that count as an accident? This time the answer was more satisfactory. Chantrelle recounted the pistol incident in greater detail and said he intended to insure himself and his wife against a fatal accident. Mr Macwhinnie suggested he should rather take out their ordinary form of policy, which offered so much for fatal accidents, and an allowance for injuries while the effect of such injuries lasted; Chantrelle was not interested; he 'evinced a desire to be covered only against fatal injuries'. However, he did not fill up a form at the time, saying that he thought he should give the matter further consideration. Instead he went to another insurance company, the Accidental Assurance Association of Scotland, where he took out three policies. One, for Mary Byrne, their servant, was for £100 in the event of death and an allowance of fifteen shillings a week during disablement. The second was in favour of Lizzie and was for one thousand pounds against accidental death only. The third, in his own favour, was in the same terms as Lizzie's.

That was in the middle of October. There were some unusual features to the transaction. First, it was rare for 'policies to be taken out in the name of females'. Indeed the manager of the Accidental Assurance Company stated that of the eight hundred policies they had issued in this the first year of operation, this was 'the first and only application of the kind'. Then the Crown was to make Chantrelle's eliciting of the information as to the exact meaning of the term 'accidental death' look sinister. It was strange that he had sought this information from one company, and then taken out policies with another – 'an office', as the Lord Advocate said pointedly, 'where he asked no questions of the kind'.

It is not too much to say that the insurance policy hanged Chantrelle. On the one hand, it gave him a clear interest in Lizzie's death (as long as it bore the appearance of an accident), and thus supplied a motive comprehensible to even the most unimaginative jury; on the other hand, if he was innocent of murder, it was to prompt him to an act of total folly. Yet there were good reasons why the thought of insurance should have occurred to Chantrelle. The pistol accident at Portobello had actually happened. He had been wounded. He might easily have been killed. So might Lizzie. So might Mary Byrne. 'Was it wonderful', as Chantrelle's Counsel asked, 'that the prisoner proceeded to insure his life and that of his wife against accident? That was the real reason he did it. It was a desperately unnatural reason to suggest that he insured his wife against accident because he wanted to kill her and make money to pay the butcher's bill.' Perhaps so; but murder, as the jury may have reflected, especially domestic murder, is itself a 'desperately unnatural' act. It was also, if Mrs Dyer was to be believed, a reason that had occurred to Lizzie.

'About six weeks before her death', said Mrs Dyer, 'she told me that Mr Chantrelle wished to insure her life in an accident insurance company. He expected, she said, to get an agency, and said he meant to insure his own life and hers as well. My daughter said she did not care to have it done; that she did not see the use of it, as she was not travelling about anywhere. . . . On the Thursday before her death she reverted to the subject . . . she said to me, "my life is insured now, and, mamma, you will see that my life will go soon after this insurance." I said, "you are talking nonsense; you should not be afraid of that; there's no fears of that." She replied, "I cannot help thinking of it; something within me tells me it will be so. . . ."'

Though asserting that her daughter seemed 'under real apprehension' the egregious Mrs Dyer did nothing. She was accustomed to Lizzie's fears; they were her old friends. She had frequently communicated her husband's threats: 'that he could give her poison which the Faculty of Edinburgh could not detect. She was serious when she told me that – under real alarm'.

Mrs Dyer had not been able to respond with equal seriousness; perhaps she was simply bored by Lizzie's apprehensions. She had cried 'wolf' too often, had been crying it for ten years, and there she still was. 'Threatened people live long' was a proverb quoted by Chantrelle's counsel, Mr Traynor. Mrs Dyer seems to have agreed. She knew her Lizzie too well to be put out by her 'real alarm' and 'real apprehension'. So she ignored her latest fears, just as she had never bothered to consult a lawyer about Lizzie's rights. Mrs Dyer was anxious to avoid acandal.

Such then was the state of the Chantrelle household at the end of the year. The family had passed a merry and agreeable Christmas, during which financial problems seem to have been set aside. Lizzie's health was generally good, though she was inclined to sleep badly. As a result sometime in December the two older boys went through to sleep in their father's room, even though they had all three to sleep in the same narrow bed.

On New Year's Eve, Lizzie was in 'very good spirits', according to Mary Byrne, whose evidence gives a clear and largely reliable account of the course of events. Her mother had sent a cake and some shortbread. She busied herself doing some shopping and playing with the children. The baby was put to bed about half-past six, and, when Chantrelle came in a little later, they all had supper with a bottle of champagne, the survivor of a pair bought for Christmas. Lizzie gave Mary Byrne a glass, but she did not care for it, and gave it to little Louis. After supper the children were put to bed and Lizzie then went out to post two New Year cards, one to her mother and the other to her friend in London, Anna Baird; she promised Mrs Baird she would write a letter in a day or two. When

103

she came back she sat with her husband in the parlour. At last twelve o'clock struck, the bands in the Castle began to play, and Lizzie called Mary from the kitchen to come into the dining-room and listen to the music. Chantrelle warned Mary not to lean out of the window – 'she might get a blow' – she thought he might have been joking. Soon after, they all went to bed. A quiet, uneventful, domestic day; in deference to the occasion, Lizzie had stayed up a couple of hours later than she was accustomed to do.

That did not seem to have affected her the next morning, for she appeared downstairs at the usual time, between half-past eight and nine. Eugene, the oldest boy, had come down earlier, about eight, with the baby, and had passed on a request that Mary prepare tea and toast. Lizzie took only one cup of tea and one slice of toast, though she usually had a bit of bacon or an egg. After breakfast she sent Eugene out to buy a duck for their dinner, and herself took the baby to the kitchen to wash him as usual. She told Mary to leave the teapot by the fire, as she would take another cup later. 'She said she had a little touch of headache, but nothing to signify.' Then, leaving the baby with the second boy, Louis, she went upstairs and into her husband's room. He said later that she had come to fetch the enema machine, which she used frequently. Towards eleven o'clock she told Mary that she could go out for the rest of the day, it being a holiday. She was to be back by ten in the evening. 'She did not complain to me, and she was not looking any different from ordinary', said Mary. Mary then spent the day with friends or family, and returned between half-past nine and a quarter to ten. Chantrelle answered her ring. He told her that Lizzie was not very well. She had felt ill after washing the baby about half-past six, and had gone to bed. Mary at once went up to see her mistress, without taking off her outdoor things. She found her, 'lying stripped and in bed below the clothes, the baby at her back'. What struck Mary about her appearance was that, 'she was very heavy looking and did not look so well'. However, she asked Mary about her day, and, speaking in her usual tone, assured her that she felt better than she had done earlier. She said she would like some milk; Mary offered to go and fetch some, but

Lizzie looked at her watch and decided it was too late – the shops would be shut. Mary noticed a tumbler of lemonade, three parts full, on the bedside table. Lizzie asked her to peel an orange for her. She did so, dividing it into quarters. She gave her one segment and put the others on a plate which already held half-a-dozen grapes. There were one or two grape skins there too. She could not tell whether Lizzie ate the piece of orange she had given her, for she now said that she was tired and would need nothing more that night. Mary left her there, with one gas lamp lit – the bracket over the mantlepiece – and, putting out the gas in the kitchen and the lobby, went to her own bed. All the time she had been aware of Chantrelle in the parlour, though she did not see him again after he opened the door for her. Next morning when she went in there to tidy up, she found a large empty whisky bottle and an ashtray full of cigarette stubs.

There are two accounts of how the day had gone in her absence, Chantrelle's and young Eugene's. In general they tally well enough, though, not surprisingly, Eugene's memory of what had happened several months before he was called on to give evidence, was not very detailed and perhaps not always exact. Nevertheless the outline of the day is beyond dispute. Chantrelle went out about noon, taking little Louis with him. His intention was to go first to the Post Office to get a postal order with which to pay his Income Tax. If true, this would suggest that his financial position was not absolutely desperate; but he may of course have claimed this was his intention in order to create that very impression. However he found the Office closed, not surprisngly, since it was a public holiday. Meeting a friend, Herr Spanier, he repaired with him to the Hanover Hotel, where he spent most of the afternoon. 'They were out a good long time', said Eugene. While they were out, Lizzie vomited, sitting by the parlour fire. 'It was like water what she vomited', said Eugene. He told his father about this when he returned and Chantrelle asked if she had drunk any champagne. She said she had not, and he then sent Eugene out for some lemonade. Later the two boys were despatched again, this time for grapes. Chantrelle told his wife that she should 'not put herself about', and that he would finish preparing the dinner.

They dined around five o'clock on duck and onions, but Lizzie took nothing. She fed the baby and then lay down on the sofa. Afterwards she said that she would wash the baby, which, as Chantrelle somewhat complacently put it, 'showed that she was able to do it'. She and the baby were in bed together by six o'clock. She seems to have dozed on and off through the evening. The boys called on her to say good night before going to bed about half-past nine; Eugene saw no difference in her appearance. Chantrelle went out briefly to Hardy the tobacconist in Frederick Street, and stayed there, by his account, till about half-past ten; he probably had a drink there too. (This story conflicts with Mary Byrne's version, though the difference is hardly important.) Afterwards he sat in the parlour with the whisky bottle till almost midnight. He went upstairs, undressed and called on Lizzie. He found her, he said, sitting up in bed. She had been reading *The Family Herald*. He stayed with her for about an hour and let it be understood that they had made love. This was probably untrue, merely an attempt to suggest that they were on good terms. It was not supported by any medical evidence; and, apart from her sickness, she was menstruating. When he left, he took the baby with him. He had said to Lizzie, 'if you like I will give him to Jack (Eugene), who is a capital nurse'. Eugene soon lulled him to sleep, and Chantrelle returned to Lizzie. He found her out of bed, 'as if she had got up for some necessary purpose'. He wanted to stay with her, but she was ready for sleep.

Mary Byrne was up early as usual the next morning, before a quarter to seven. She went straight to the kitchen and set about getting water for tea for her mistress, but when she was crossing the parlour (where she observed the empty whisky bottle) to get coal and sticks to light the fire, she was arrested by a strange sound. She described it as, 'a moaning like a cat's'. It was repeated two or three times. First she thought it came from the street, but then traced it to Lizzie's room. She was surprised to find the door open and the gas out; both occurrences were unusual. Lizzie was lying near the edge of the bed, partly on her side, partly on her back. The bedclothes were thrown half off, and her head had slipped off the pillow. There was no sign of the baby. Mary Byrne thought her mistress 'awfully pale-looking'; 'she had never seen any person in that state before'. She noticed 'a green brown-like stuff on the edge of the pillow and bed, like vomit'. She shook Lizzie, but, getting no response beyond the moaning, went through to the other room to call Chantrelle. She was surprised to find all the children in bed with him. 'There was scarcely room for them in the small iron bed.' Chantrelle got up at once, came through to his wife's bedroom, and knelt beside her. He asked Mary if her mistress had spoken. Mary said she hadn't and suggested that he should call a doctor at once. At that moment Chantrelle raised his head, apparently hearing something in the next room; he sent Mary through to see if the baby was all right. She obeyed of course, though she had heard nothing herself.

When she returned to say that the baby was sound asleep, she found Chantrelle 'coming from the direction of the window, as if after raising the bottom sash of the window'. He now asked her if she didn't smell gas. At first she could detect nothing, but in a little found the smell quite strong, though not what she would call 'a suffocation smell'.

Chantrelle now set off in search of a physician, having instructed Mary to test the gas at the bracket and then turn it off. He called on Dr James Carmichael of Northumberland Street, not the nearest medical man. The family had no regular doctor, since Chantrelle, with his claimed expertise, was accustomed to treat their ailments himself, and maintained a well-stocked pharmacopeia. He knew Carmichael however, as a fellow Mason. He gave a message to Carmichael's servant and hurried home. Carmichael arrived about twenty-past eight. He had had to dress, but since his servant had given him the message at seven-forty, and Northumberland Street is at most seven minutes walk from Chantrelle's home, he had hardly made remarkable speed.

Carmichael was sufficiently impressed by the smell of gas, even though the door and window had been open for some time, to insist that Lizzie be moved through to the other bedroom. Not unnaturally he prepared to treat it as a case of gas-

107

poisoning. Being inexperienced in such cases, he sent a note to Dr Henry Littlejohn, the Police-Surgeon, whom he knew to be interested in such matters. He also sent Mary Byrne to get a bottle of brandy, and used various methods to try to resuscitate Lizzie's breathing. These included the administration of an enema of brandy. All efforts were in vain, but Carmichael soon noticed that the brandy was beginning to disappear 'though neither Madame Chantrelle nor myself took any'. A medical student, George Harrison, who resided with Carmichael and who came along later, about a quarter-past ten, at his request, found that, 'Chantrelle had drink upon him'. When he arrived, Chantrelle was sitting by the bed, holding his wife's wrists; he did not seem very excited.

By this time however Dr Littlejohn had already arrived. He had one advantage over Carmichael, and a sore one it was for Chantrelle: he had some knowledge of how things stood in George Street, having been involved with both of them before. That had been on the occasion of Chantrelle's arrest; then, Lizzie and her mother had called on the police surgeon to say that Chantrelle's conduct 'was such as to make her suspect his sanity'. Now, although Littlejohn did not suspect that gas might not be responsible for Lizzie's condition, his special knowledge made him alive to what might be the implications of her state. At first, he had thought Lizzie already dead; then he was certain that she would not recover. He considered it therefore imperative that her friends should be there, and asked Chantrelle if his mother-in-law had been summoned. Chantrelle, who, understandably, had no desire to see Mrs Dyer in the house, claimed that he did not know her address. Littlejohn had no time for such nonsense. Young Eugene was despatched to fetch his grandmother. Littlejohn went further however. He said that in his opinion Lizzie should be removed to the Royal Infirmary. Chantrelle made no objection, and Littlejohn left on other business, sending word also to the Gas Company that they should inspect Chantrelle's house. At this time he considered gas-poisoning 'the only possible explanation'.

Mrs Dyer arrived, accompanied by her family doctor, Dr Gordon, who had come however in the capacity of a friend –

not that that made much difference. He later claimed to have come to the immediate conclusion that Lizzie's symptoms indicated narcotic, rather than gas, poisoning. If so, he does not appear to have imparted his suspicion to anyone else at the time, for when Lizzie was admitted to the infirmary at about a quarter to two, it was as someone suffering from gas-poisoning. She was immediately examined by the celebrated Dr Douglas MacLagan, Professor of Medical Jurisprudence at the University. He found her, 'lying totally insensible, with the muscles relaxed, and the pupils of the eyes somewhat contracted. She was incapable of being roused; the respiration was interrupted and the heart's action was scarcely discernible. The pulse of the wrist was not to be felt . . : the heart's action was so feeble that he had to use his stethoscope to hear whether it beat or not . . .' Moreover, and more importantly, when MacLagan applied his mouth and nose closely to the patient, he could detect no smell of gas. He concluded therefore that it was rather a case of narcotic poisoning, possibly opium or morphia. He remained with Lizzie for about an hour, applying artificial respiration, the interrupted current of a galvanic battery, and giving her another enema of brandy.

Chantrelle arrived at the infirmary while this was going on, and was told that the case was now regarded as one of narcotic poisoning. He asked MacLagan if he knew they had had an escape of gas. That was all his conversation with the doctors, but he flew out at Mrs Dyer, telling her that they were murdering Lizzie by their treatment. He had a low opinion of other doctors, and particularly of the infirmary. Years before he had told Mrs Dyer that they had murdered her husband there; now it was his wife's turn. He said he could not remain there to watch them do so, and stormed out, to return home. Mary Lethbridge, a nurse in the infirmary, described him demonstrating that the gas meter was broken and the dial running round, by making a circle with his forefinger. She had thought him reluctant to approach the bed, and she did not think he showed much anxiety about Lizzie. By the time he returned just after four, Lizzie was dead; everyone else had gone. He had returned home in the meanwhile, given the maid money to buy food for the children's dinner, and finished the brandy. It must have been a bitter hour. Apart from other considerations, the abandonment of the gas theory would certainly mean the refusal of the insurance company to accept Lizzie's death as accidental; and so, bang would go the thousand pounds he so desperately needed. But perhaps the brandy clouded his perceptions for the moment, and he did not yet realise this.

Meanwhile, having laid aside the gas theory, the doctor now started to explore the possibilities of other forms of poisoning. They soon fastened on opium. That raised difficulties. Post-mortem examination might reveal the cause of death, but, again, it might not. As Dr MacLagan was to say. 'it is a very rare thing to discover chemically traces of opium at all in the body. It is, I believe, from the length of the fatal illness in opium poisoning that we do not find it. Some of the other vegetable poisons that we find kill more rapidly ... every poison is absorbed into the system, but this one disappears in the system.' That was a real problem. Certainly Lizzie's symptoms were consistent with opium poisoning, though some things that might be looked for were absent; on the other hand they were by no means inconsistent with coal-gas poisoning – even the disappearance of the smell of gas could be accounted for by her exposure to a pure air, in which the smell could be expected to dissipate itself. However, there were other means at hand. Lizzie had vomited, and her nightdress, the sheets and pillowcase on which she had been lying, all bore the stains of her sickness. These might yield evidence to analysis, and, the police, who had been early alerted, took possession of them. It was to be urged, on the other hand, that Chantrelle had had ample opportunity to remove them and destroy the evidence, an opportunity which he had made no attempt to seize; equally, it was eventually to be suggested that others, especially Mrs Dyer, had had the chance to tamper with them. There was to be some uncertainty as to which stains were present at which time.

It was also necessary to establish the cause of the escape of gas, for that there had been one was undeniable, though it might not perhaps have been the cause of death. A gasfitter was sent round by the Company on Wednesday, 2 January, in

response to Dr Littlejohn's note. He established the fact of an
escape, and that it did not come from the meter. He then made
no further inspection: 'we are not allowed to make any inspection if the escape is from internal fittings. The householder in
that case makes the inspection himself; it is only for escape at
the meter that the Company is responsible', he explained,
giving a good example of the working of demarcation prac-
tices. Accordingly, since Chantrelle took no action himself to
determine the cause, a criminal officer, William Frew, requisi-
tioned two other gasfitters from the Company, and examined
the flat on the Friday. They were not long in finding the cause.
A bracket had at some time been removed from the architrave
of the window. The fitter thrust his hand behind the shutter
and found a loose pipe. They then searched more thoroughly
and discovered the corresponding pipe lying on the floor.
Both pipes had been sealed up, but the end of one piece had
been wrenched off. The fitter gave it as his opinion that, 'it
could have been done very rapidly . . . you could do it in two
turns back and forward'.

The inference was clear. Chantrelle had come into the bedroom when summoned by Mary Byrne, concluded that Lizzie
was dying, and at once, thinking of the insurance money, had
sent Mary out of the room on the excuse that the baby was
crying. In her absence he had torn off the end of the pipe, and
allowed the gas to escape. It was the work of a moment. Even
so, Mary had met him coming away from the window. Chantrelle denied any knowledge of the pipe's existence. This
denial was easily shown to be false. In August 1876 it happened that a gasfitter had been summoned to investigate an
escape of gas in the same bedroom, and had discovered that it
came from this same pipe, which had been inefficiently sealed
when the bracket was removed. At the time Chantrelle had
said that 'he had not been aware that there was a gas pipe
behind the shutter, and that it must have been that damned
dirty German.' It was assumed that he referred to a previous
tenant. In any case the plea of ignorance could hardly be con-
vincingly repeated.

There could be little doubt that Chantrelle had broken the
pipe, and that he had done so in the hope of collecting the in-

111

surance money. Yet this explanation left a good deal unaccounted for. It did not necessarily mean that he had murdered Lizzie. It convicted him of callousness more certainly than of murder, and it was clumsy and unintelligent. Yet it nearly came off: Lizzie was treated for gas-poisoning, and was admitted to the infirmary on that basis. Neither Carmichael nor Littlejohn doubted this diagnosis, though Littlejohn's knowledge of the Chantrelle family made him naturally suspicious of the cause of the escape of gas. And therein lay the measure of the stupidity of Chantrelle's desperate effort, for it took only a minimal investigation to establish that the gas had been released from the broken pipe, and that the break could not have been accidental. Accordingly, if Lizzie's death had actually been caused by the gas, or if this had been accepted as the cause of death, it seems likely that the immediate case against Chantrelle would have been more clear-cut than it actually was to be. It could be established that he knew of the pipe behind the shutter, and that he had the opportunity to break it and the motive to seek an accidental explanation of Lizzie's death. In every way then the action was stupid, so much so that it is hard to believe that Chantrelle was in his right mind.

Probably he was not. The empty whisky bottle presents itself for consideration again. Assuming, for the moment, Chantrelle's innocence, it is easy to reconstruct what happened. Roused from sleep by Mary, he wakes, his faculties still blurred by drink, to an immediate realisation that, somehow or other, for a reason he cannot establish, Lizzie is dying. At once the thought of the insurance money presents itself to him, and the memory of his conversation about the definition of accidental death flashes through his mind. In particular he recalls Mr Macwhinnie's insistence that, 'there must be outward and visible sign – an ascertained cause of death'. An accident must therefore be fabricated. He sends Mary from the room, and does the job, with no thought of probability, but acting rather with the confused brilliance of the drunk.

What if he was guilty? What if he had indeed, as the Crown was to insist, poisoned Lizzie with solid extract of opium. In this case too a satisfactory explanation is not hard to seek. He had all along intended to create the impression that gas was the cause of Lizzie's death, since there could be no certainty that death from opium poisoning would be accepted by the insurance company as accidental, and it must be insisted that he had no other motive for killing Lizzie. (To suggest that his frequent threats provided such a motive, was merely silly, as his Counsel was to point out. Apart from his urgent need for money, he had no reason to murder Lizzie that he had not always had; arguably, less.) All he had to do then was wait until Lizzie was sufficiently doped by the opium, wait, that is, till she had lapsed into insensibility, and then turn on the gas at the bracket without lighting it. (Mary Byrne found it unusual that the gas was out – she had never found it like that before.) That had been the plan: to slip back into Lizzie's room, and turn the handle, gently flooding the room with gas, so that, when Mary came to wake her, the cause of death would never be doubted; that was why he had removed the baby, an unnecessary action otherwise. But, fuddled by whisky, he forgot or bungled the job – no doubt the timing was a matter of nice discrimination: enough gas to suggest the cause of death, but not enough to stupefy him and the children in the next room. Perhaps he lay down for a moment, and passed out.

He must then have been astonished and distressed in the morning to find no smell of gas in the room at all. There, on the one hand, was Lizzie, certainly dying from the opium; here, on the other, was 'no outward and visible sign – no ascertained cause of death', and consequently, no insurance money. In the circumstances he had to think and act quickly. It was no good turning on the gas at the bracket now; that would be the first place Mary would check, and it could never admit enough gas before then to be credible. So, getting Mary out of the room, he attacked the pipe. It was the only hope of salvaging his plan, the only way in which he could ensure that there was at least a credible quantity of gas released.

That decision was the last autonomous one for Chantrelle. Henceforth he was at the mercy of others' interpretation of events. He had not long to wait. Suspicion gathered quickly. The post-mortem examination took place on Thursday, 3

EUGENE MARIE CHANTRELLE

January. The broken pipe was discovered the next day, Chantrelle on that date still maintaining to Mrs Dyer and his brother-in-law John James Dyer that Lizzie had been killed by gas. He suggested that the pipe might have been broken by the children hanging their clothes on the shutter, an absurd theory. He was by now disturbed by the police activity. Mary Byrne described him coming into the kitchen on the Thursday evening with a bottle, a tumbler and the watercrock. 'He began to speak about the officers, and he wondered very much what they were wandering about the place for. "I wish they would give me peace", he said, "and leave me alone. . . . Do they want to make out that I poisoned my wife?"' He had reached that moment which comes to murderers when they realise that they are no longer free agents: consequences, long ignored, will have their inexorable way. The paradox is revealed. The murderer kills to realise his power; up to the moment of action his power, being only potential, is enormous. He kills, and feels himself at one with the Gods. But the Gods are jealous and animated by irony. From that moment, his freedom is curtailed. Power, actualised and no longer potential, drains away. Subsequent actions, even successive murders, are forced on him: 'to be thus is nothing, but to be safely thus'.

The post-mortem examination by Professor MacLagan and Dr Littlejohn had failed to establish the cause of death, but had confirmed MacLagan's opinion that it had not resulted from coal-gas poisoning. (A subsequent chemical analysis was also to yield no positive evidence.) However the analysis of the stains on the nightdress and bedclothes revealed the presence of opium. Though they could not show how it had been administered, the Procurator-Fiscal judged that the circumstances of the death, the results of this analysis, and the history of the marriage combined to justify Chantrelle's apprehension. He was therefore arrested on the afternoon of Saturday 5 January, immediately after Lizzie's funeral, during which he had displayed an emotion which impressed those present. He was taken to the Calton Jail, examined in the City Chambers on the Tuesday and Wednesday of the next week, and lay there awaiting the preparation of the indictment against him.

That took some time and it was not till Monday 8 April that Chantrelle was served with it. It substantially bore that on 1 or 2 January he had murdered his wife in his dwelling house by administering opium to her in orange and lemonade; and it further bore that he had previously evinced malice and ill-will towards her, and by his maltreatment and threats had previously put her in fear of losing her life. Appended to this document was a list of 115 witnesses and an inventory of 198 productions, many of which were to be irrelevant.

Two points may be made about the indictment. First, it was clear that the Crown had been unable to decide how the opium had been administered, for it was absurd to suggest that he had doctored both orange and lemonade. (How you stuff opium into an orange sitting on someone's bedside table is a bit baffling too.) What they were doing was leaving an escape route. This fuzziness was to be a handicap for the Defence, who never seemed quite certain exactly what they were arguing against. In fact, Mr Traynor chose to dispute the cause of death, the coal-gas therefore acting as a screen in a way ironically opposite to that intended by Chantrelle. So much time was to be spent in disputing the cause of death that the Crown's failure effectively to establish the means of administration was never satisfactorily challenged.

The second part of the indictment was fuzzy also, for the full text referred to accusations of adultery and incest made by Chantrelle against his wife. These could only confuse the argument, for though it might be an essential part of the Crown's case to show that relations between the two had never been good, to introduce these matters was to risk irrelevance and prejudice, since it was never proposed that jealousy had been a motive for the murder. The Defence therefore objected to their inclusion. Yet the removal of those words did not remove the fuzziness. It was the Crown's case that the motive for the murder lay in Chantrelle's financial position and in the insurance policy: but a good deal of the evidence led was rather calculated to show what an unsatisfactory husband he had been. In other words it was designed to blacken his character, or perhaps, more fairly, to reveal the black side of his character, so that the jury might believe him capable of a murder which the Crown otherwise doubted its ability to prove he had actually committed. It was if the whole tenor of the Crown's case was calculated to distract attention from the act of murder, and direct it towards the character of the accused. And nobody pointed out that all this evidence might have provided Lizzie with a motive for murder rather than Chantrelle; for surely the abused wife has more reason to kill, than the husband who abuses her.

The trial opened on the morning of Tuesday 7 May. It was raining, but that did not deter a huge crowd from gathering in Parliament Square, some of them hoping for admission, others content merely to boo and hiss the prisoner. So great was the throng that the Police had to exercise force to clear the approaches for those who had the right to enter. It was no wonder. As W.N. Roughead put it, 'in the Edinburgh of the late Seventies the Chantrelle case created a painful sensation . . . the aspidistras shuddered in their chaste receptacles.' 'It was', in *The Scotsman*'s words, 'the only such crime committed in the city by a man of education in the last fifty years.' Chantrelle had been in many a correct drawingroom; men of substance and standing had known him as a fellow Mason.

In the dock he looked languid and weary. He had spent four months in prison, and was still wearing mourning. Such proprieties had to be observed, just as Lizzie had been buried in her wedding gown. His voice was calm and self-possessed as he made his plea of 'not guilty'.

The trial was to last for four days, of which three were taken up by the evidence and the fourth by the speeches of the Counsel, the Judge's charge to the jury, and the verdict and sentence. Inevitably the Crown with its huge list of witnesses took up most of the time. In contrast the Defence only called eight witnesses, one of them being the Crown witness Professor Maclagan, recalled for further questioning; the Defence had to rely therefore on counterpunching. A good deal of the Crown case was occupied with the Chantrelle marriage. The theory of suicide was quickly dismissed. Lizzie, it was said had never indicated any desire to kill herself (Chantrelle's assertion that she had, made in his Declaration, was never referred to; probably wisely.) Moreover her card to Anna Baird had promised a letter in a day or two; that did not sound like suicide. Finally her devotion to the children made the whole idea absurd. The question of the cause of death resolved itself into the choice of coal-gas or narcotic poisoning. Much of the evidence was therefore highly technical, and it may reasonably be questioned whether the members of the jury were able to follow such detailed and frequently contradictory exposition; or to retain it, if they did. Even reading the evidence is hard going. Probably they relied on the Judge eventually elucidating it for them, and telling them what they should believe; he rather shirked doing this; correctly enough. The nub of the Crown case here was that though the post-mortem examinations showed no opium in the body, the stains on the nightdress and sheets showed opium clearly. In other words, though they could not prove that opium had stayed in the body, they could show that some of it had come out; and, of course, Lizzie was dead, which was, to say the least, evidence of something.

Chantrelle's part in her death was still difficult to prove. He had of course considerable knoledge of the uses and effects of poisons. He had opium in his possession – a drachm (60 grams) of solid extract of opium which he had bought on 25 November 1877. This was, the Lord Advocate said in his summing-up of the crown case, 'about twenty or thirty doses, each sufficient, if administered, to prove fatal to human life. He (the Lord Advoate) did not know whether it was suggested that the prisoner was in the habit of dispensing that drug. There had certainly been no explanation as to what came of that opium. It was not found anywhere in his house. The extract he bought in 1872 was got in the press; but the extract bought in November was not there, and what came of it he did not know. But what, after all, was the evidence that he dispensed? Did doctors use that amount of opium in such a time? . . .' That certainly sounded a formidable argument, and it may be imagined that jury-heads wagged in assent. Opium bought; opium not to be found; opium therefore in Lizzie. All the same the Defence had an answer, for it turned out there was another bottle in the press, labelled no 24 in the

Crown's list of articles, and this was a fluid extract of opium. So Mr Traynor was able to say that, 'it was just as obvious as that two and two make four, if a man would open his eyes and look at the fact, that that was what came of that drachm of opium. It had been reduced to a fluid, and that was where it had gone to . . .' Only, there remained the question of quantity, and this was never resolved. So, after much argument, no one was really any the wiser.

The Crown was however on surer ground elsewhere. There was Chantrelle's attempt to create a false impression of the cause of death; there was the breaking of the gas pipe; there were his foolish protestations of ignorance as to the pipe's existence; there was the fact that Mary Byrne had noticed no smell of gas when she first entered the room; there was the fact, the sort of fact which is always significant, that Chantrelle had been the last person to see Lizzie on the night before she died, and that he had, by his own account, given her lemonade and a piece of orange. And then, in a grand finale, the Lord Advocate rehearsed yet again the miserable circumstances of the Chantrelle marriage, the story of Chantrelle's violence and of his frequent threats to poison Lizzie in a way that could not be detected; and he asserted incontestably 'that the prisoner was interested to the extent of one thousand pounds sterling in the woman's death being accidental, that, and Chantrelle's indigence, were facts that could not be argued away. They would help the jury to believe that, because Chantrelle was a bad husband, it followed that he was a murderer also.

It was a strong case for the Defence to answer. Their own evidence had been so thin that Chantrelle had given vent to a cry of despair from the dock: 'is that all the evidence for the Defence?' Still it was not impregnable, and Mr Traynor knew it. He began by reflecting, as one reasonable man to twelve others, on what had been said about the Chantrelles' daily life.

'They heard that Chantrelle did not often take his meals with his family, that he did not sleep in the same room as Madame, that he did not rise early, that he had a cup of tea taken to him in his bed. Now the Jury knew, he durst say that these were but the ordinary habits of a Frenchman's life...'

This was good man-of-the-world stuff, flattering to the jury. Mr Traynor proceeded to dismiss the threats and the violence in the same sort of tone. Chantrelle might be a bad husband; there were many worse ones, 'who kicked and abused their wives as Chantrelle never did, who would yet shrink from the attempt to take away their lives.' Even infidelity and the frequenting of brothels were not, in Mr Traynor's tolerant view, evidence of intent to murder one's wife. He went so far as to suggest that anyone who believed otherwise was, 'not fit for anything else than a residence in Morningside.' (He meant, one assumes, the lunatic asylum rather than the genteel suburb, though possibly that might be the conviction of the suburb too.) He pointed out, moreover, that relations between Chantrelle and Lizzie had improved in the eighteen months before her death. 'It was suggested by the Lord Advocate that he commenced to treat her better (after 1876) so that he might poison her in 1878.' That Mr Traynor considered 'a most extravagant suggestion.' This was the voice of reason; but reason had more difficulty when it came to considered the financial aspects.

True, he was able to show, or at least suggest, that Chantrelle's need for money had not been urgent when he had actually taken out the insurance policy. He was able to exercise effective sarcasm as to his presumed intention with regard to the other policy holders – did he mean to murder them all? But none of this was ultimately convincing, for he could not hide the fact that Chantrelle's financial position had become desperate since: there were the letters from the Union Bank, pressing for payment, the last one (dated 27 December) threatening that, unless payment of the balance of his bill, was made by the end of the month, they would, 'institute proceedings against you for recovery of the Debt'; there was the evidence offered by John James Dyer that Lizzie, 'said her husband was in pecuniary difficulties, that he owed over £200, and that he had nothing to pay it with'.

Finally, though Mr Traynor made a determined attempt to

confuse the cause of death, and to suggest that Lizzie had indeed died of coal-gas poisoning, that still left unanswered the question: 'Who broke the pipe?' No one could imagine that this had been done by anybody other than Chantrelle. The whole irony of the case rested there. If coal-gas had been accepted as the cause of death – which was what Mr Traynor was still striving to suggest – then there would have been absolutely no difficulty in proving Chantrelle guilty. At best, one feels, Mr Traynor must have been hoping for a verdict of Not Proven; and he might get that if he had sufficiently obfuscated the intelligence of the jurymen.

The Lord Justice-Clerk, in his charge to the jury, dwelt first on the nature of circumstantial evidence, on which the case wholly depended. He said, 'circumstantial evidence, when it is complete, is as satisfactory as any evidence can be. A combination of circumstances, all pointing, and pointing clearly to one cause, will produce conviction on the minds of men as readily as direct evidence . . .' He took the jury through the evidence scrupulously, with fair balance. Nevertheless his gist was clear enough: the case turned on the casue of death: if the jury felt opium poisoning had been established, then they had no option but to convict Chantrelle, for, that granted, all the circumstances pointed to his guilt. (But, of course, if the doctors and the Crown had gone for gas, and they might well have, the same would have applied.) Only if the Crown had failed to make out that case could he escape.

The jury were out for an hour and twenty minutes, long enough to suggest that they had heeded the Lord Justice-Clerk's advice that they should go over the reports of the post-mortem examination, and of the chemical analysis of the sheet and nightgown. Their foreman, an Edinburgh surveyor, announced, 'the jury unanimously find the panel guilty of murder as Libelled.' The time taken and the unanimity (majority verdicts have always been permissible in Scotland) indicated clearly enough that they had had no serious doubts about convicting a man on circumstantial evidence. Their position almost certainly was that, on the evidence led, no other explanation could account for Lizzie's death. It is unlikely that, even if it had been possible for Chantrelle to have gone into the witness box, he could have led them to believe otherwise. He would have made a disastrous witness: glib, cocksure, ready with the evasive or irrelevant reply, he reeked of untrustworthiness.

The Lord Justice-Clerk passed sentence. Chantrelle was to be hanged on 31 May. Hardly had he stopped speaking when Chantrelle indicated that he wished to make a statement. What he said was extraordinary enough. He completely ceded the Defence theory of gas-poisoning. It had never perhaps seemed adequate to him; now, having had leisure to think, he saw it could serve no further purpose. Away with it therefore. Instead, after some palaver and compliments to the jury on their close attention, he said:

'I am willing to admit that the dark stains on the sheet and on the nightgown – and allow me to say that I am speaking not so much in my own interest (a man has only one life and I have sacrificed mine) – but I am speaking in the interest of public morality and public safety; and I say I am willing to admit that these stains on the sheet and on the nightgown contained sufficient evidence that opium was there. I go further: I say opium was there; I am satisfied that opium was there. I am satisfied, further, gentlemen, that I did not put it there; that it did not proceed from Madame Chantrelle's stomach; that it was rubbed in by some person for a purpose I do not know. I know my word goes for nothing. I don't wish it to go for anything. My reasons for saying this are these: opium was administered or taken in a solid form – that is perfectly evident. If there was opium there it was in the solid form. We see it with the naked eye. The analysis might not be sufficient. The reactions of meconic acid and the reactions of morphia, especially from the chemist's point of view, may not be satisfactory, though satisfactory from the common sense point-of-view. But how could the reactions of morphia and opium have come there accidentally? When we find the smell of opium and the bitterness of opium, which is certainly very characteristic, looking for opium, it is quite enough . . .'

EUGENE MARIE CHANTRELLE

So thought the Lord Justice-Clerk. Quite enough, and more than enough – it was a wonder he had let him go so far. 'I think you had probably better not proceed further at present.' Still he had started a hare, one that would run. It was probably unwise, and certainly ironical, to have used the expression 'from a common sense point-of-view'. A common sense point-of-view, that precisely described how the jury had come to their verdict. It was hard to say positively, on the strength of the evidence, that Chantrelle had killed Lizzie, harder still to say that the Crown had thoroughly proved its case. In the long run, that was not so important. Not for nothing had Edinburgh been the home of the common sense school of Philosophy, for when you came down to it, that was what operated here. Common sense could devise no other explanation for Lizzie's death. Common sense said that Chantrelle, the jealous, alcoholic, violent, needy, unprincipled frequenter of brothels, had done for his wife.

There could be no appeal, but it was possible to address a petition for mercy to the Home Secretary. (The Office of Secretary of State for Scotland did not yet exist.) Chantrelle himself drew up a memorial, which his solicitors transmitted to Whitehall. Meanwhile, a public petition, praying for commutation of sentence, was also forwarded. This drew the Home Secretary's attention to the purely circumstantial nature of the evidence, to the fact that no evidence of opium was discovered in the body and that, 'when opium was discovered on the sheet upon which the deceased lay, which sheet however had been in the possession of various persons, including the prisoner's mother-in-law . . . crude stains of opium were discovered upon it. This stain, while it was verified to contain crude opium, was never verified to have been in the stomach of the deceased . . . further, the experienced infirmary nurse swore that the dark opium stain was not on it, and was distinct from the other vomits upon the other linens, which other vomits were found to have contained no opium whatever.'

The petitioners then elaborated a case which had a close resemblance to Chantrelle's: 'a similar case of suspected poisoning was demonstrated by a careful post-mortem examination to have been only a case of kidney disease . . . the patient was a married woman of about thirty years of age, whose life had been insured for a large sum only some six months previously. Her husband was in great poverty. The case was under the care of Dr Sutherland, who was so struck by the symptoms in the case, that he called in the aid of an independent physician, . . . who, without any collusion, at once expressed a similar opinion that the case was one of poisoning. Dr Littlejohn, already referred to as a Police Expert, was then applied to, who expressed a similar conviction, notwithstanding that no poison could be detected in the urine which was submitted for examination. In a few days she died, when a joint examination, where the husband's interests were represented, laid bare beyond the possibility of dispute that the case was one of undiagnosable kidney disease . . .'

So they suggested that Lizzie had likewise died of natural causes, that Chantrelle, entering the room when summoned by Mary Byrne, at once perceived that she was dying, and that, 'the evil thought then occurred to him for the first time how he could turn her death to his account. To cheat the Accidental Assurance Company was the evil suggestion. . . .' In support of their theory, the Memorialists stated that it was, 'inconceivable had the prisoner poisoned his wife by opium that he should have retained in his possession for four days the damning evidence in the stains upon the sheet, which he had ample means of destroying, on the one hand, while, on the other, he had a perfect knowledge that an inquiry was going on against him.'

This was spirited pleading, and it attracted vociferous support. It posited a combination of accident and malice, amounting to conspiracy, and there are always those, possessed of a constitutional dislike for the obvious, who will hasten to embrace conspiracy theories. It could hardly be called satisfactory, for the three legs on which it rested were all shaky. First, it suggested that someone, probably Mrs Dyer, had stained the sheet with opium to implicate Chantrelle; that was of course the essence of his outburst in court, but there was no evidence whatsoever to support it. Clearly, it could have happened and Mrs Dyer had certainly no reason to wish Chantrelle well; but it remained no more than an interesting assumption. Second, the theory assumed that an innocent Chantrelle had recognised at first glance that Lizzie was dying when he entered her room in the morning; that was a quick diagnosis indeed. Third, the parallel case proved nothing. The kidney was a red herring, for in the report of the post-mortem examination it was stated that, 'the liver and kidneys were congested, but otherwise, both they and the other abdominal organs were healthy'. It did not seem then that Lizzie had died of kidney disease.

Conspiracy theories and the like are better able to excite the idle than convince the responsible; and so it proved in this case. The Home Secretary could discover no reason to commute the sentence. Not even a last minute public meeting, held, appropriately enough some may think, at the Oddfellows Hall, could influence his judgement: Chantrelle must die.

He received the news stoically. 'If it is to be, it must be', he said. During the period of waiting he had earlier shown a sour misanthropy. A warder reported him as saying ('between clenched teeth' as befitted his role) 'Would that I could but place a fuse in the centre of this earth, that I could blow it to pieces, and with it, the whole of humanity. I hate them.' In the same spirit he had refused the ministrations of a Roman Catholic priest. Now, however, he made the customary obeisances to religion, confessing that he had led an evil life, but asserting that, deep down, he had always had a sense of the majesty of the Almighty. In the same correct and resigned manner, he accepted a decision that an interview with his children would be inexpedient. All this was very gratifying; it is, as we have seen, not only proper but pleasing to the conscience that the condemned to death should be seen to admit the error of their ways, and return with full penitence to the faith of their childhood. It makes the whole business of executions seem less like an act of revenge. In Chantrelle's case it was all the more remarkable because he never admitted that he was guilty of the crime for which he had been sentenced.

This was all very decorous, though the old Adam was not

yet dead. Asked by the Governor, the night before his execution, if there was anything he would like to have, he replied: 'send in three bottles of champagne and a whore.' The request was denied, and he shrugged his shoulders. It certainly has his authentic tone, even if it does not wholly accord with the lengthy statement he had handed over to the prison chaplain earlier in the evening. Then he had spoken of resting his hopes on Jesus; but he had also taken the opportunity yet again categorically to deny the murder. Everyone knew, he said, the love he had for his children; he could never have harmed their mother, and he wished them distinctly to understand this.

So, having asserted innocence, and been denied his whore, he slept soundly still he was woken at five. He prayed with the chaplain, breakfasted on coffee and eggs and a glass of brandy, and smoked a cigar. He still wore his suit of mourning. He was then pinioned by Marwood the hangman and conducted to the room of the chief warder where a short religious service was held. At the end of this, the chaplain made a final solemn plea, that he should now confess anything which he had hitherto denied. He declined to do so.

The execution was the first held in Edinburgh since Parliament had decided that Public Executions belonged to a coarser age. Nevertheless, a crowd had assembled, in bright sunlight, on the Calton Hill, hoping to be able to catch of glimpse of proceedings. They were disappointed. Things were so arranged that the procession – bailies, clergy, warders, prison governor, victim and hangman, – had only to cover some fifty yards, out of sight of the watchers, to an outhouse on the western side of the prison, which had been selected as the place of execution. The floor of the outhouse formed the roof of a deep cellar. A trap door, railed off with a low black screen, had been cut in the floor in such a way that, when a bolt was drawn, it gave way and was kept down by two sand-bags. The scaffold itself consisted of a cross-beam, between two uprights about seven feet high. A hook was attached to the beam. The rope hung from the hook.

It didn't take long. Chantrelle watched calmly as the last adjustments were made. Everyone was impressed, and probably relieved, by his tranquillity. The chaplain began to recite The Lord's Prayer. While he did so, Marwood withdrew the bolt; and that was that.

Jessie King

Or the Fate of Bastards

There was an army of them; over 20% of the population of
Edinburgh, according to the 1881 census.

They got up early in the morning, six o'clock perhaps, and
began cleaning, polishing the black-leaded kitchen ranges,
scrubbing the front door-steps and the area; down on their
hands and knees, scrubbing the stone flags of the kitchen;
sweeping and polishing the diningroom where the family
would take breakfast; tickling the cornices free of cobwebs
with long feather dusters. Soon it was bathtime for the family;
in relays they would carry bucket after heavy bucket of hot
water up three, four, five flights of stairs; or perhaps, before
then, they had already carried hot water for shaving or washing, or tea-trays to the bedrooms, where they withdrew the
curtains, opened the shutters, tidied the clothes, and in
winter, cleaned out, relaid and lit a fire. If it was winter, then
there were downstairs fires to be raked out and laid (though
never fires from May to October) great scuttles of coal to be
filled from buckets carried all the way from the cellars in the
area below the level of the street. Whatever the season the kitchen range had to be stoked and coal brought in for that. All
day there was cleaning, and washing in the great tubs in the
sub-basement, and ironing, and fetching and carrying and
waiting on the family; work in the kitchen, work in the
bedrooms, work all over the tall steep house with its hundred-
and-fifty stairs from bottom to top. Of course there were
lighter moments: meals in the kitchen, quick exchanges of
gossip and chat with the various tradesmen and itinerant ven-
dors who called at the house – the fishwife from Newhaven
who always had a wealth of news, the coalman, the butcher's

cheeky boy, the postman, the grocer's delivery man, they all kept the household in touch with the life of the streets. But still, much of the time, in the chaste squares and crescents of the New Town, or the tree-shrouded villas of the Grange and Morningside, the servants, almost all female, led secluded secret lives.

The young girls waited for the evening when they might be permitted to slip out for an hour or two, or for Sunday when they were sometimes free in the afternoon between church services. In some households they had a half-day off once a week, or perhaps once a fortnight. Of course prudent employers, mindful of their duties to their dependents, would catechise them on their return, seeking to discover how they had passed these few hours of dangerous leisure, when, as everyone knew, Satan might find mischief for idle hands. (It was presumed, no doubt correctly, that the employers themselves, though frequently idle, were possessed of a moral robustness that served as a guard against the devil's wiles.) But there were of course households where the mistress was less particular, or there were girls who had the ability to deceive and few scruples about doing so. These were high-spirited maids, or simply weak, in thrall to the flesh or responding heathily to natural desire. It did not really matter how it was put. They were girls who, on their brief excursions from Service, excursions which might take them to the dance hall, the public house, to some waste piece of ground, or for a walk along the Water of Leith or in the windy expanses of the Queen's Park by Holyrood, contrived to get into trouble.

Within a few months evidence of their sin, evidence of their shame, would be apparent. What happened then took on a divergent pattern. Sometimes their young man was respectable and willing, sometimes even in a position to propose marriage. That would mean a change of status, a change of way of life, but no impairment of their respectability – many a good marriage was celebrated with the wife months pregnant. Sometimes the girl had a mother, aunt, or married sister, who would look after the baby and make herself responsible for the child's upbringing. Sometimes a gin-or-whisky-sodden midwife performed a crude and dangerous abortion. If that happened, then the girl would probably only have to change her post; it might be possible simply to give out that she had been ill. Sometimes in a dark corner, a nearly-crazy girl, her mind turned by shame, fear and the execrations hurled at her by family, employers or upper servants, would stifle the infant whose existence seemed the cause of her distress. Sometimes she threw the child on the parish or left it wrapped up on a doorstep. Sometimes she advertised the infant for adoption or care. There were always plenty of applicants. The whole thing was all too common. Over 7% of births in virtuous churchgoing Edinburgh were illegitimate.

Three girls who found themselves in this predicament between the Spring of 1887 and September 1888 were Catherine Gunn or Whyte, Violet Duncan Tomlinson and Elizabeth Campbell. All were domestic servants. All were brought to bed of unwelcome children, bastards for whom respectable society offered nothing. All had themselves a respectable position to maintain. They never met, but they all had this in common and were linked more particularly by the solution they sought.

Some solution, however desperate, had to be found. All had families who were not prepared to take on the child, and they could do nothing themselves. Elizabeth Campbell died in childbirth. Violet Tomlinson was maddened by the strain and shame, and consequently confined. Only Catherine Gunn survived, demure in the black uniform and starched cap of her trade. 'Witness was in domestic service and could not keep the child.' What was to be done?

In the case of Elizabeth Campbell who had died in childbirth, her sister looked after the baby from May 1887 to August, when the seducer, being known, was persuaded to take up his responsibility. He was not long in acquitting himself of it, for he straightway advertised for foster-parents. A couple presented themselves, a little woman in her late twenties and a man some thirty years older. The woman said the man was her father and that their name was Stewart. Finlay, the seducer, then gave Stewart £5 and the baby. He considered that he had done his bit; £5 was a tidy sum with

129

which to launch his bastard on the world. He also handed over the child's birth and vaccination certificates, and he recommended to the Stewarts that they should not let the Andersons (the baby's uncle and aunt) know where it was. Doubtless he considered that this injunction would save him any possible trouble in the future.

The Stewarts took the child to their lodging in Dalkeith Road, where they were known by the name of Pearson. They had not been together long, and were not of course father and daughter. Pearson, Mike to his acquaintance, was a big bald dirty grey-bearded man, of indeterminate age, but certainly at least fifty. He described himself, from time to time, as a labourer, though in the period when anything is known of him, from May 1887 to February 1889, his labour was intermittent. The woman was called Jessie King or Kean, of Irish extraction, a Roman Catholic. In Court she appeared to the dramatic Roughead, whose first case this was, 'mean, furtive, shabbily sinister, like a cornered rat'. Those who saw her in more ordinary surroundings found her unremarkable. Their landlady at Dalkeith Road, Mrs Penman, said she had seen them both the worse for drink. It was a bond between them.

Why they took the name of Stewart on this occasion, and why they pretended to be father and daughter, were questions never determined. Natural duplicity, guilt even before the act, may be advanced as a reason at least as probably as any imputation of premeditated villainy. Pearson was anyway careless as to which name he used, often calling himself Macpherson. In court he was to be asked why he had used so many names. 'How many?' he replied. His explanation of the name Macpherson was revealing; it stamps his type. 'I have gone under the name of Macpherson since I was a boy. I used to go to Highland gatherings, and Macpherson was an appropriate name to take at such gatherings. They would find (he continued) his name in *The Scotsman* of 1857 as the winner of a first-class prize. . . .' *The Scotsman* of 1857 . . . it was then 1889, and here was this great dirty drink-sodden lout harking back over thirty years to his moment of glory. Perhaps his first-class prize had sustained his self respect these three decades.

130

Of Jessie's past nothing is known. She had taken up with Pearson that May, when he had lodgings in Gifford Park. They stayed six months at Dalkeith Road. The baby was seen by various neighbours as well as Mrs Penman. One of these, formerly a nurse, looked after it on occasion, and found it a fine healthy infant. Then it disappeared, was simply no longer in Jessie's possession. 'She had sent it away to its aunt'; that was the explanation given, but no aunt ever received the baby. No one saw it again. Its body was never discovered. The £5 were, one assumes, exhausted.

Pearson and Jessie removed to Ann's Court, Canonmills, where their landlady was a Mrs Mackenzie. They were living there when, sometime in the Spring of 1888, Alexander Gunn was acquired. Elizabeth Gunn had borne twin sons, who for some months had been looked after by a nurse called Mrs Mackay. For reasons never explained it became difficult to continue this arrangement. Accordingly Alexander's availability was advertised, and out of twenty-nine replies received, Jessie was selected. One wonders what the other twenty-eight applicants were like, that they should have appeared manifestly inferior to her. She now called herself Mrs Macpherson, and this time received only £2 with the child. She told her landlady that, 'it was the child of her husband's sister and her own brother'. It was surely a superfluous lie, the unnecessary precision of detail also marking her as an habitual liar. The nurse, Mrs Mackay, had some conscience, perhaps also some affection for the child. She called at Ann's Court in April or May and found all well. Again Jessie had begun successfully. She was making an effort to look after Alexander, even though her landlady had had occasion to check her for giving the baby spirits: 'the child was crying when she poured whisky over its throad'. However, she employed the daughter of a neighbour called Burnie to nurse the baby; Janet Burnie looked after him each day from ten in the morning till six at night. Perhaps Jessie had taken a job; certainly Mike Pearson had begun to work about a month after they moved into Ann's Court.

However, one morning when Janet arrived, she found no child. This baby too had simply disappeared (not that Janet had ever heard of the Campbell one of course). Mr Macpherson told her, 'the child was away across the water for the good of his health'. When Mrs Mackay called round again that September, the Macphersons had departed also, leaving no address. They had in fact moved to Cheyne Street, Stockbridge, where they had taken rooms, still under the name Macpherson.

By now, September 1888, Jessie was pregnant herself. Her condition did not stop her from responding to another advertisement, this time from Mrs Tomlinson. Violet, Alice's mother, who had been in domestic service, was now in hospital, leaving a bastard on her mother's hands. Jessie's tender was accepted by the baby's grandmother as 'being the lowest', evidence of the old lady's tender affection. Jessie said she wanted the child for her sister, Mrs Macpherson, 'who was married to the Duke of Montrose's piper'. This was a flight of grandeur indeed, possibly in honour of Macpherson's glorious past.

She took the child back to Cheyne Street in a cab. Isabella Banks, her landlord's daughter, saw them arrive. Jessie threw the child up in the air, caught her at the full stretch of her arms, pulled her down to her face, and held her tight there. 'My bonnie wee bairn', she crooned. She asked Isabella to hold the child while she paid the cabbie, and then took her back, saying that the baby's mother would come soon. She asked the girl to go out and buy some beer. Isabella never saw the baby again.

Nor did anyone else. Jessie told Mrs Banks that she 'had put it away', and she told James Banks, 'that she had got a child and £25 to keep it; and that she had given it and £18 away'. The Bankses did not question any of this at the time, though the three of them had each been told a separate story, but there were other circumstances which made them feel that the Macphersons were not entirely satisfactory lodgers. The disappearing child was strange enough in itself, especially as Mrs Banks one day saw a baby's hat on Jessie's bed. Whose was it, she asked, and found herself less than convinced by Jessie's assurance that it was part of the layette for the baby she was herself expecting; perhaps she could not believe that this slatternly and drunken couple would be exercising such forethought. Then there was the case of the coal–closet which the Macphersons obstinately kept locked. On one occasion when Mrs Banks asked for the key she was displeased to find it refused. Jessie made the excuse that the closet was full of dirty clothes. Finally, Mrs Banks claimed to find something suspicious in the fact that Mr and Mrs Macpherson 'had a private and peculiar chap' (knock). This is another example of how literally almost anything can be made to seem suspicious and sinister in a Court of Law. There can be few married couples who do not have similar private signals of recognition; it is something which establishes the special nature of lovers' relationships, like the use of pet names; but it sounds grim in a trial. Quite clearly, if the Macphersons had their 'private and peculiar chap', it was evidence of a guilty secret.

That they, or at least Jessie, had such secrets was soon to be apparent. But first Jessie left to have her baby and returned without one. Presumably it was stillborn or had died almost at once. That could have surprised nobody: of 394 deaths in Edinburgh the following February, 63 were of children of under one year. Certainly this child disappears completely, the note that Jessie went off expecting to be confined being the only record of its existence.

Then on 26 October a group of boys were playing around Cheyne Street. On the narrow and muddy green they discovered a parcel rolled up in a waterproof coat. One of the boys kicked it, thinking it was an old pair of boots. The kick was oddly squidgy. Investigation revealed the body of a child. They went to the police at once.

Their find was examined the next day by Sir Henry Littlejohn, still Police Surgeon, and Dr Joseph Bell, most celebrated as one of the originals of Sherlock Holmes. They discovered it to be a male child, about a year old. The body had been wrapped in an oilskin and was partly mummified. There was a ligature round the neck. The cause of death could not be exactly established, but the presumption that it was strangulation was obviously strong.

The news of the find alerted and alarmed the community of Cheyne Street. Fortunately nobody there, or in the streets immediately around, had recently lost a child, so that the search

133

had all the thrill of the race without any of the concomitant anxiety. Horror rather than pain was the dominant note, one much more easily endured, even indeed rather enjoyable. Joseph Banks however was inevitably suspicious of his lodgers. They behaved mysteriously. There had been a child in their possession and then it had vanished. Now the body of a child had been found. Either its sex had not yet been revealed or, more probably, Mr Banks had never known that the Tomlinson baby, which had made so brief an appearance in his house, was a girl, for he immediately assumed that the body on the green might be the baby his daughter had seen arrive in the cab. He went to the police.

They acted quickly on his information. A Detective Officer, James Clark, called upon Mrs Macpherson. He asked her what had become of the baby she had brought there in the cab. She produced a pair of baby's shoes, for no reason that one can think of, and stated that the child was now with her sister, the wife of the Duke of Montrose's piper; as if the noble connection would give ballast to her tale. Clark was not satisfied however. He had been told of the coal-closet; the Bankses were certain this was a suspicious circumstance. He said he would have to make a search.

Jessie broke down straight away. 'Get a cab, it's there', she sobbed, pointing at the closet. This must have surprised Clark, who presumably at this time was hoping merely to find something in the cupboard that would connect Jessie with the body on the green. He opened the closet. 'On the bottom shelf was the body of a female child wrapped in a canvas cloth.' Littlejohn and Bell's subsequent examination established the age – six weeks – and that 'the lower part of the face was tightly enveloped in cotton cloth'. Again the cause of death could not be absolutely established; either suffocation or strangulation was possible.

There was still more, however. On the top of the cupboard Clark saw a horrible corresponding mark, the stained outline of a small body. Clearly the other baby, the one found on the green, had lain there; this was Alexander Gunn. The little girl, Alice Tomlinson, who had been wrapped in layers of newspaper, cloth and oilskin, had been dead since September;

Alexander since April or May. Alice had died here in Cheyne Street, Alexander in Canonmills. He had formed part of the Macphersons' luggage when they flitted.

Jessie was taken to the Police Station. Macpherson (or Pearson) soon followed. She made no comment in her first declaration, while he, possibly an old hand at these matters, denied everything. Next day however she made a second declaration in which she admitted the two murders with which she had already been charged.

This declaration was clinching. Her admissions to Clark had no force binding in law, but the jury would be expected to take her declaration into account. As the Lord Justice-Clerk put it at her trial: 'In this country persons were not subjected to what they were subjected to in other countries, namely to have every scrap of conversation they might have with police officers and other officials brought up in court'. (That was a hit at English practice of course). However, since the Criminal Procedure (Scotland) Act of 1887,' a prisoner, in emitting a declaration was entitled to have the assistance of a law agent' and any admissions made in such circumstances were legally valid. This meant that Jessie's declaration could by itself put the rope round her neck.

Still she made an effort to put the best construction possible on what she had perforce to admit. She denied intent. She had been very pleased to have the Gunn child, but by the end of May they had found themselves unable to support him. The £3 she had received with him was exhausted. She had tried to have him admitted to a home, but she had been refused because the child was illegitimate. (This may have been true.) She was in despair. Whether she had made any attempt to approach the baby's family by way of Mrs Mackay was not stated; the presumption must be that she did not. At any rate, one Monday, 'when very much the worse for drink', she had strangled the child. Pearson had been out at the time; he had known nothing of the death. She had wrapped the child in an oilskin and hidden the body in a box, which had later been transported to Stockbridge with them.

The Tomlinson death had been accidental. She had given the baby whisky to stop her crying and had overdone it. The child had been killed and, in a panic, she had concealed this body too. Feeling perhaps that the closet was over full, she had taken out the Gunn boy and exposed his body on the green. This was an action as stupid as it was macabre. The Green lay just outside her door, a mean bare spot, where no body could hope to lie concealed. The stream of Water of Leith runs some three hundred yards away, and, though certainly shallow and frequently choked, might yet seem a more sensible place of hiding. Even if for some reason she had decided against the Water, one would have thought that she might have had the sense to go farther from home. A body found in Cheyne Street was sure to promote questioning around, and, even though there was no, or at least little, ostensible connection between the Gunn baby and Stockbridge, certainly no evidence that he had ever been there, yet the disappearance of the little girl might be fresh in people's minds. Any police investigation was likely, one would think, to lead to the Macphersons. That this simple line of argument does not appear to have occurred to Jessie may be taken as the full measure of her stupidity; just as the place of concealment in the coal-closet is evidence of her moral insensibility.

She was charged with three murders, there being sufficient suspicion attached to the Campbell baby also. The Prosecution were to drop this charge eventually, since there was no body and no evidence of death; it had at least the advantage that the baby's father, David Finlay, who had so callously felt he could shed his responsibilities at the cost of £5, was exposed in the witness box to public obloquy and judicial reproach. Jessie never admitted responsibility for this death, but there can be little doubt that the wretched child died while in her hands. Since his death was never registered, the assumption that he went the same way as the other two is not likely to be challenged.

The trial itself was a foregone conclusion. Interest lay in the horror of the circumstances, in the appearance of Jessie and her lover, and in the evidence given by Pearson. Roughead, whose first case this was, compared the pair to that great scene in *Weir of Hermiston* when Hermiston is faced by the wretched Duncan Jopp and his miserable paramour. This comparison invests the Macphersons with the glamour of great literature; the Stevensonian echo can be heard in Roughead's prose:

> 'The miserable little creature in the dock – mean, furtive, shabbily sinister like a cornered rat; her truculent robust paramour, with his dirty, grey-bearded face and his bald head, upon which a monstrous wen, big as a hen's egg, rose eminent on his naked scalp.'

Since we have already been told that he was bald, the 'naked scalp' is a piece of superfluous information, but it undeniably enhances the description's operatic quality. Roughead has of course stopped short of any Romantic idealisation of the murderess (for he was certain that Macpherson, 'that some-time ornament of the Highland Games', as he calls him with superior irony, was every bit as guilty as Jessie; indeed the likely instigator.) One could go further indeed, and say that Roughead's tone places the wretched pair with something of the same Augustan contempt that Cockburn offered Haggart. Nevertheless there is a note of glamour here: murder is some-thing exciting; murders have something 'sinister' and 'mon-strous' about them. This obscures the fact that murderers are often, in the first instance, rather people who are incompetent at living; Jessie King certainly was. Of course, if you are going to hang someone, it is more satisfactory, morally a good deal more acceptable, if you can present him as a mon-ster rather than be compelled to recognise him as a miserable derelict or simply a moral defective. Which is not to say that the act of murder is not itself unspeakably horrible, that the revulsion felt from the murderer is not proper; but horror lies also in the waste, emptiness and the wilderness of the mur-derer's inadequacy as a human being, in the failure of any sympathetic imagination.

Jessie gave no evidence, but all the little pieces contributed by the landladies, the nurses, the relatives who had handed over the babies, the two girls, Isabella Banks and Janet Burnie, and finally by the detective James Clark, built up a picture of a wretchedly incompetent person. She should never have been entrusted with a baby, not so much because she was evil – she was very doubtfully that – but because she was weak, shifty, lying, drunken and incapable. There is no real reason to suppose that she took on these babies as a callous commercial enterprise, killing them off as soon as the money was exhausted; she would hardly have employed Janet Burnie to look after little Alexander Gunn if that had been her attitude. The most vivid picture in the case is that offered by Isabella Banks, of Jessie emerging from the cab, throwing the six-week old Alice Tomlinson into the air, then pressing her against her cheek, as she crooned 'my bonnie wee bairn'. Impossible to dismiss this simply as glutinous and revolting sentimentality and hypocrisy; the horrid possibility presents itself: Jessie King really liked babies; she was just no good at looking after them, and could not cope with the demands they made. It may be that each time she thought it would be all right; this time there would be no hideous accident, no moment when she found the effort intolerable.

Pearson's evidence was vivid and interesting. He stood there in the witness box rather than the dock in the finest tradition of that style of justice which is always prepared to reward one scoundrel that another may be hanged. He was *socius criminis*, there to consign his crony to the gallows, as Hare had done for Burke. Only this time, one might think, there was a difference, and one which renders the whole business even more obnoxious. Jessie's declaration, though exculpating Pearson, was sufficient to incriminate herself. One wonders therefore why no more determined attempt was made to press the case against Pearson. Certainly Roughead, from the gallery, had no doubt that he was the dominant partner. It may have been felt however that an attempt to convict Pearson would invalidate Jessie's confession, and that somehow or other both would contrive to cheat justice. It was better not to risk it.

Accordingly, Pearson stood there in the box, heavy-shouldered, pot-bellied, obsequious and yet powerful. He was informed by the Lord Justice-Clerk that, as he had been put in the box to give evidence, he could not be charged with anything arising out of proceedings there, except perjury; and he gave a quick furtive little lick to his lips, meanwhile darting small bloodshot eyes around. Oh yes, he remembered Alexander Gunn being bought. The child seemed about a year old, but he knew nothing of its parentage. He had had no objection to Jessie's keeping it. Only, after a bit, well, there was a shortage of money. She had spoken of getting the child into a home – Mrs Stirling's Home for Children in Causewayside. (There was in fact no such home there, but a Miss Stirling did keep a Home in Stockbridge. Whose lie this was cannot be established – it sounds like Pearson distancing himself from the action.) Well, the child had gone, and she had said it was in the Home. He had wished to visit, but Jessie had put him off, saying male visitors were not allowed, or only on certain days. Why had he told Janet Burnie that, 'the child had been sent over the water'? He had understood that children from Miss Stirling's Home were sent to Canada; that was what he had meant by over the water. Oh yes, he had several times expressed a desire to take the child a present. Jessie had then told him he could see Alexander running about Causewayside in a blue gown. This ridiculous flight of fancy on the part of the aged athlete – Alexander being then barely a year old – was allowed to pass unchallenged; possibly Counsel was struck dumb by his matchless effrontery. So much for Alexander: Pearson had of course been absolutely ignorant of the contents of the boxes which he had transported from Canonmills to Stockbridge, and it was Jessie kept the key of the coal-closet.

The cross-examination was not rigorous. The money from Finlay and Mrs Mackay had gone on keeping up their house; he was sure of that. Then came the matter of his names. His 'how many?' speaks volumes. Pearson/Stewart/Macpherson was absolutely ready to account for anything and everything that the police already knew; it was though first a matter of making sure just how much they knew, so that he might learn what he had to account for. Then he launched himself forth, but the judge, hitherto indulgent, stopped him before he could expatiate further on his athletic achievements; he stood down and lumbered out of the Court. Did he give Jessie a backward look? Had he glanced at her while he secured the rope round her neck?

The verdict was a formality. The jury were out for only

four minutes. She was sentenced to be hanged on 11 March, just three weeks ahead. 'All that you have done', said the Lord Justice-Clerk, 'can be blotted out, if you will but repent and turn from it. Listen, I beseech you, to the ministrations you will receive. . . .' She can of course have expected nothing else, but she can never have sufficiently imagined what it would feel like in experience. 'Her face', wrote *The Scotsman* reporter, 'became ghastly pale and she gave vent to repeated groans of the most heart-rending description.' She had to be carried fainting from the court-room.

Her mood in the next few days was suicidal. Roughead, with odious irony and a callousness which he was accustomed to attribute to his murdering subjects, wrote: 'Twice or thrice she tried to commit suicide by strangling herself with strips torn from her skirt, and similar improvised ligatures. But her hand had lost its cunning, for she was less successful than in her previous essays in thuggery.' How nice, one may reflect, to know what thuggery really means, and to be superior to guilt, misery and despair. Fortunately for Jessie, and indeed for decorum, she had those about her who could fortify her. A Roman Catholic priest, Canon Donlevy, and two Franciscan nuns, were constant in their ministrations. She came to some peace of mind as a result; her despair seems to have been transmuted into penitence.

An agitation for a reprieve was started in Stockbridge. Feelings perhaps ran less high there than might have been expected considering the revolting nature of the crimes, if only because none of the little victims came from that quarter itself. The public, sensitive to the position of a woman, in an age which made a cult of feminine virtues, was disturbed by the promised execution. Even the foreman of the jury sent a telegram to the Secretary of State: 'Don't like to interfere with the administration of justice, but if there is any ground for further investigation, let accused have benefit.' There was of course no such ground; the only further investigation that could have made sense would have attempted to establish the guilt of the unspeakable Macpherson; and that was prevented by the immunity he had been granted. (Connoisseurs of the criminal mind may like to ponder the contrast between Macpherson, willing to let the woman he had lived with hang that his own skin might be saved, and the notorious Ned Burke, who, as Owen Dudley Edwards has shown in his recent study, devoted his own Defence to the exculpation of his mistress, Helen MacDougall. Yet Burke is a synonym for villainy, while Macpherson/Pearson is unknown.)

Meanwhile, *The Scotsman* recognised the changing mood of the public, its susceptibility to the gentler and more humane emotions. In an unusually thoughtful leader, the newspaper looked forward to a time when a softening of public taste might mean that the public would 'demand for its own sake rather than that of the criminals fully and justly convicted of taking away life, that Capital Punishment also shall be a thing of the past.' That was prescient; we have arrived there today, the strongest case against capital punishment resting on its deleterious and debasing effect on the public imagination and on the odious excitement it so easily generates. It is after all the block, the gallows, the electric chair that give a ghoulish glamour to murder.

That time had not yet come and there were no grounds for a reprieve. None of the doubt that surrounded the Chantrelle case existed on this occasion, and there had been no suggestion that Jessie was not responsible for her actions, though it was recognised that she was 'of a low moral and intellectual type'.

The morning of 11 March dawned bright and frosty. The hangman was the celebrated Berry. A group of sightseers had assembled on the Calton Hill – 'of a motley character, largely composed of idlers and loafers' – in the hope of getting at least a glimpse of the procession to the scaffold. Within the prison, emotion and tension ran high. Several of the female warders showed 'eyes red with weeping'. By contrast Jessie was now calm, supported still, as she would be right to the end, by Canon Donlevy and the two nuns. Since public executions had been abandoned, it had been customary to allow the press in to view proceedings, on the grounds that, otherwise, some people might remain unconvinced that the execution had in fact been carried out. At the last moment however it was decided that, following a recent English precedent in the case of the execution of a woman, the reporters should not be permitted to view the actual drop. This information was conveyed to the press as the procession was even on its way to the gallows. Some of the reporters would have challenged it, but they felt that a prolonged or vigorous altercation at that moment would be insensitive; accordingly they gave way and remained behind in a little room. The last they saw of Jessie, she was walking blindfolded, with a crucifix held before her, as Canon Donlevy recited the litany. They heard her say with him, 'Christ have mercy upon me . . .' A few moments later they heard 'the dull thud of the drop'.

They were then allowed to pass through to the execution chamber. Canon Donlevy was still standing by the edge of the drop, his eyes closed, his lips moving in prayer. Berry, 'an unwashed looking figure, had struck a reflective attitude, and was gazing, chin on hand, down upon the body. "She has never moved since the drop", he said, *sotto voce*.' They looked down. The crucifix was still clutched firmly in her hand.

At about that moment, or perhaps a little earlier, Catherine Gunn – 'witness was in domestic service and could not keep the child' – withdrew the heavy velvet curtains of her mistress's bedroom, and commented on the fine bright spring-like weather. Her black dress rustled as she closed the door behind her and tripped briskly down the long flight of stairs to the basement.

Of course the case provoked argument and recrimination. What it revealed of the callous traffic in infants, of the carelessness with which they were cast out into the world, of their wholly unregulated disposal, was disquieting and discreditable. *The Scotsman* remarked that, 'in foreign countries – in Naples for instance, there are Foundling Institutions where deserted children, the offspring in most cases of guilty passions, are cared for and brought up. . . .' But, the writer felt, and doubtless the good sense of respectable Edinburgh would have agreed, that this was hardly the answer. Did not the existence of such institutions serve as a support, even an encouragement, of vice? Who would feel the need of continence and chastity if they knew that a Foundling Hospital existed to receive and rear the fruits of sin? Such reasoning might

be specious – the twenty-nine applicants for Alexander Gunn
had shown that disposal of the fruits of sin presented no difficulty as it was; yet, for all that, the reasoning was not without
force.

Nor, one must admit, did it lack prescience:

'The scandals that occasionally arise in connection with that
saintly institution, the Foundling Hospital at Naples, are
enough to make humanity shudder. Of 856 children living
under its motherly care during 1895, 853 "died" in the
course of that one year – only three survived; a wholesale
massacre. These 853 murdered children were carried forward as still living, and the institution, which has a yearly
revenue of over 600,000 francs, was debited with their
maintenance, while forty-two doctors continued to draw
salaries for their services to these innocents that had meanwhile been starved and tortured to death. The official report
on these horrors ends with the words: "There is no reason
to think that these facts are peculiar to the year 1895". . . .'

Norman Douglas: *Old Calabria*, Note, pp.72–3

Such a report makes Jessie King seem small beer, a
wretched amateur, a tyro.

Donald Merrett

Or the Pike Swims Free

There is a style of writing about Edinburgh so common as to amount to cliché. Essentially it consists of drawing a contrast between the Romantic Old Town and the Classical New. The writer describes, frequently in hectic tone, and always in lurid hues, the pell-mell conditions of life as it clung to the spine of the rock running from the Castle to Holyrood, with all its dirt, squalor, vivacity, the bohemian taverns and contiguity of classes, in short its feverish intensity. The New Town on the other hand, lying across the deep divide of the old Nor' Loch, is portrayed as cool, chaste, restrained, elegant, bourgeois. The adjectives pile up endlessly. Then perhaps the writer goes on to dramatise the contrast in terms of Deacon Brodie (who pursued his double life exclusively in the Old Town), Jekyll and Hyde, doppelgangers, even perhaps, if he is of a unusually literary turn, the Caledonian Antizyzygy. It always makes an impressive and entertaining passage. There is something in it too. The move of the middle classes from the Old Town did denote more than a geographical exodus. It was a first step towards changing the character of the city.

Nevertheless it is possible to overstate the contrast; and this for two reasons. First, while the advocates, doctors and professors mostly removed their residences to the New Town, where they would almost all be found living by 1830, the situation of the Law Courts in Parliament House, and of the university and infirmary, meant that they passed their working lives in the intense, even foetid, atmosphere of the Old Town. As for the advocates, who did so much to give the tone of the city, many of their clients, at least at the Criminal Bar, were necessarily drawn from the wynds and closes that clung to the

145

skirts of Lawnmarket, High Street and Canongate; they themselves continued to spend hours in the taverns around St Giles. There could, in these circumstances, be no absolute divorce of Old and New.

Second, the New Town itself was less of a piece than the cliché would have us believe. This is particularly true of its eastern end, where lanes housing artisans' workshops thread their way between the backs of terrace and squares. There was more of a social mix than might be at first apparent. Cumberland Street and the now vanished Jamaica Street, for instance, were never without their artisan inhabitants. The bourgeois quarter drifted almost imperceptibly, around Broughton Street and Leith Walk, towards Canonmills and Stockbridge, into streets where prostitution and crime were common. After all Jessie King had lived and killed not far from prosperous terraces like Inverleith and Ann Street. In the same way, farther up the hill, the correct imposing boulevards, Princes Street, George Street and Queen Street, were divided by sordid alleys where vice was for purchase. The Chantrelle case had revealed brothels in Clyde Street, just round the corner from the banks in St Andrew's Square.

It is in detail, timing, exact geographical distinction, rather than in essence, that the contrast is misleading. Undeniably the perceived character of Edinburgh changed between the eighteenth and twentieth centuries, so that distinct aspects of the city, tending towards schizophrenia or a double life, are recognised. The colloquial summary of that character − 'fur coat and nae knickers' − may be too condensed; it is at least an attempt to catch the paradox that many have discerned. How did Auld Reekie become, 'East Windy and West Endy'? How did the tumultuous city of 'Gardy-loo' become known among other Scots for its genteel and refined frigidity?

The answer is not to be found in the New Town as such, which, despite its classical façade, retained so much of the rich mixture of the eighteenth century city. The clue however lies in that summary − 'East Windy and West Endy'. One must look to the West End, to the terraces and squares built beyond Charlotte Square, the Queensferry Road and the Dean Bridge, to find this restrictedly correct, almost exclusively middle class denial of the sordid and seamy; a denial which is primarily an attempt to simplify life. And one must look to a later period than the time when the New Town proper was built. Absurd, on reflection, to suppose that the Edinburgh of Boswell, Scott and Cockburn could have bred such a mood or style of living. It had to wait till later, till after the Regency, the Railway Age and the exuberant period of early Victorian expansion, till there was a sufficient diffusion of a *rentier* class wedded to the pious virtues of evangelical Christianity and domestic decency. Nothing shows this more perfectly than Buckingham Terrace and the Merrett case, which took place there as late as 1926.

Buckingham Terrace, shielded from the traffic of the Queensferry Road by a row of trees and a secondary access road, even today breathes an atmosphere of gentility, characteristic of the whole area. It is a part of town where life insists on its privacy and respectability; it goes with Turkey carpets, kidneys for breakfast and roast mutton; the terrace is tall, withdrawn and curiously silent. There is no street life, it is detached from the traffic and there are no shops in a wide area around, though, nowadays, the terraces opposite, some fifty yards away on the other side of the Queensferry Road, have been turned into private hotels. Built around the middle of the nineteenth century, these houses, demanding, commodious, yet in no way elegant, fit homes of Edinburgh Forsytes, were, even by 1918, losing attraction and being converted into flats; flats which attracted widows, the honourably retired, or spinster ladies. There they indulged in bridge, tea-parties and the gentle gossip that delights in tracing remote family connections and in the most modest and correct speculaltion about neighbours and common acquaintance. Nowhere in Edinburgh, not even Morningside, was more respectable. It was this quality, more than anything else, that was to lead to what was almost certainly a miscarriage of justice in the Merrett case.

Mrs Merrett was a newcomer to the terrace. She was the daughter of a prosperous Manchester wine merchant. In 1907 she had married a New Zealander, John Alfred Merrett, an electrical engineer. Their only child, Donald, was born in New Zealand in August 1908. Soon afterwards they moved across the world, to Russia, at that time, in the last ten years before the First World War, engaged in the most rapid economic expansion of its history. There Mr Merrett, whose conduct at least suggests considerable enterprise, took a job in St Petersburg. His enterprise may have been combined with a difficult character, for the marriage did not last long. Soon Mrs Merrett was living apart from her husband, in Switzerland; then later in New Zealand again. Nothing more is known of her husband. She was to tell her maid in Buckingham Terrace, one Rita Sutherland, that she had had a hard life and had lost her husband in the War. Her sister, Mrs Penn, later affirmed however that Mr Merrett was still alive and working in India. However that might be he made no further contribution of any kind to his family. Fortunately Mrs Merrett had been comfortably provided for by her father; she had in fact a little over £700 a year, which represented a competence, if no great wealth.

She was devoted to her only son. Donald was in certain respects growing up fast. At the age of sixteen he was tall (well over six foot), manly, bright; but difficult. No doubt he was spoiled, allowed too much of his own way. The relationship between a doting mother and an only son is always fraught. This one was no exception. Donald was indulged, yet carefully watched over; he grew up demanding and deceitful.

Mrs Merrett brought him back to the United Kingdom in 1924 and sent him first to Malvern College. Academically he did well enough – he was quick and superficially mature. His conduct however was a good deal less than satisfactory. He took ill to discipline and he had little of the respect for the conventions and traditions of the school which was demanded of him. Malvern was then an excessively correct place; nowhere were upper lips stiffer or the done thing more exactly circumscribed. Merrett, a mocker, egoist and rebel, was immune to the charms of the public school spirit. After a year his mother took him away; no one was sorry.

What she thought of him at this time, and of the school's failure, can only be surmised. At any rate, acting apparently on the advice of family or friends, she determined that Donald should no longer proceed to Oxford as had been the original intention. Life there would offer him too much freedom. It was better that he remain under his mother's watchful eye; a Scottish university would be preferable and Edinburgh was chosen. It was non-residential and he could live with his mother. Her only care being for her son, she resolved to move to Edinburgh and set up house with him. The wisdom of this course was doubtful, however well-intentioned; it almost invited rebellion of some kind.

He was however entered for the bye-term beginning January 1926. Mother and son came to Scotland at Christmas time, spending the festive season at the Melrose Hydropathic, not perhaps the most exhilarating choice for a youth of Donald's temperament. In Edinburgh they lodged first at a boarding house in Palmerston Place before renting the flat in Buckingham Terrace. Nothing could more exactly place Mrs Merrett's utter respectability than these addresses. Her landlady at Palmerston Place and her acquaintances in Edinburgh concurred in finding her worthy of them. For Mrs Sharp, the landlady, 'Mrs Merrett was "a cheerful and bright woman, a person of methodical habits."' She never saw her 'in an excitable state', praise indeed. One of her friends said that 'everything she did, she did to perfection.' She knew how to behave.

The flat she had taken was small but sufficient, a conversion on the first, or drawing-room, floor. It consisted of a sitting-room and bedroom to the front (the two rooms being carved out of the old drawing-room), and another bedroom, the kitchen and bathroom to the rear. Between the sittingroom and the kitchen was a small lobby, formerly the space between or behind the double doors which would have opened from the drawing-room to the dining-room or master bedroom behind. In the manner of such conversions the result was convenient enough, though the rooms were oddly proportioned, with broken cornices and, to the front, an unnatural and ugly division. The lack of elegance was doubtless compensated by the good address and the absence of anything in the immediate neighbourhood that could distract the boy from his studies. There was no maid's room, but Mrs Merrett was happy to see to some of the domestic chores herself, and engaged a young woman, Rita Sutherland, married but separated from her husband, to come in on a daily basis. They took possession of the flat on 10 March. Mrs Merrett, with several friends in the city, settled down to quiet domesticity and the enjoyment of her boy's university years. She wrote, to her bankers, saying 'Donald is doing well at the University and is quite settled down to the life here.'

He had certainly settled, but the university had seen little of him. He found the work boring or pointless, and his fellow students, at that time mostly the well-behaved products of the city schools, limited and unambitious. Donald asked for more from life than the round of lecture room and library, the absorption in the family life, and rugby, hockey, cricket and tennis parties that satisfied these decent young men. He required more too than the ten shillings a week which his mother allowed him. He wanted to live; oh dear, yes, he wanted to live.

His conception of life was not in fact frightfully demanding. It revolved round motor bicycles and an establishment in Picardy Place called the Dunedin Palais de Danse; there he found his true garden of delights. Roughead's Victorian good taste might shrink from what he termed 'this dreadful designation'. Many would have agreed with him, seeing the proliferation of such establishments – the *Edinburgh Evening News* regularly carried front-page advertisements for seven or eight Palais – as a mark of the godless decadence of the post-war generation. Amongst such places – and the Palais de Danse was to the nineteen-twenties what the discothèque has been to the seventies – the Dunedin was by no means the least reputable. Its advertisements combine novelty with restraint: an 'exhibition of the latest dance from America', for instance 'the famous "Black Bottom", demonstrated by Miss Vena Simpson and Mr J B Ingram'. The famous comedian, Tommy Lorne, was 'the colossal attraction' at the annual Pantomime Ball held during Donald's trial; music was provided by Pete McGovern and his Westminster Band. Lessons were given in new dances, Charleston as well as Black Bottom, and enthusiasts could learn varieties of tango, waltz and foxtrot. A still more restrained note was struck by the announcement that 'Special Thé Dansant Tickets may be had on entrance, and will include a Dainty Tea served in the popular Café Rouge'. No establishment that offered that staple of Edinburgh existence, the Afternoon Tea, a 'Dainty' one at that, could be wholly given over to vice and debauchery. Though its advertisements also promised that private rooms could be hired, the Dunedin was respectable enough, a place where Edinburgh's wellborn youth could flutter their wings a little. The widow of a celebrated novelist remembers being taken there by a would-be beau, subsequently a QC; she was fifteen and he bought her her first glass of sherry. It was clearly a place to impress a girl.

Other girls might be found there, the professional hostesses or dancing partners. Not necessarily tarts, they were nevertheless a good deal more tarty than the girls most of their customers were likely ever to have encountered elsewhere. Donald's fancy was called Helen or Betty Christie. Knowing nobody in Edinburgh, indifferent to (perhaps shy of, perhaps despising) his fellow students, whom anyway he had hardly seen, he made her his closest friend. Probably she did not represent anything very important to him, but she was a playmate. He soon made a habit of booking her out. This cost him thirty shillings for an evening session, fifteen for the afternoon, the sum paid in lieu of the dances she was missing. He gave her presents, nothing very lavish, a couple of rings valued at £2 and £2.5.0. He took her out on the motorbike with which he had provided himself by putting down a deposit of £28. (He was to tell the police his mother had bought it for him; a thoroughly improbable tale.) As for Miss Christie, she regarded Donald as 'a big romping boy'. They were 'good pals' – an expression with an exquisitely period flavour, conjuring up an image of short skirts, cloche hats and a young man dressed in the manner of Harold Lloyd. (Donald had in fact some resemblance to that comedian.) Donald made another friend at the Palais also, a young man called Scott, who doubled as clerk and dancing instructor. Scott's shallow worldliness – he owned a motor car – impressed young Donald. Flanked by Scott and Miss

151

DONALD MERRETT

Christie, he was a match for anyone, the very picture of a man of the world.

He financed this chosen life in the simplest way. In those days, before credit cards, when bankers liked to know their customers and were yet, in a curious way, more trusting, Mrs Merrett had made financial arrangements for her stay in Edinburgh which sound slightly complicated and rather strange now, but which were then simple and usual enough. Her main account was with the Midland Bank at Boscombe in Oxfordshire, to which by long-standing arrangement the cheques from her father's trust, which represented the great part of her income, were paid. In Edinburgh she had now opened another account with the Clydesdale Bank, which she financed by cheques drawn on her Midland Bank account; it was agreed that she could draw on this new account to a limit of £30. The arrangement suited her staid, regular and careful way of life.

Donald found it satisfactory too. Between 2 February and 17 March 1926 he contrived to milch his mother of £205, not far short of a third of her year's income. His method was simple. He would draw money on forged cheques made out to himself from the Clydesdale Bank, and replace this money with Midland Bank cheques. As long as his mother's credit in Boscombe remained good, and he was careful not to overdraw at the Clydesdale, he was safe. No doubt the day would come when the first of these conditions no longer could be satisfied, but that did not immediately worry Donald; a lily of the field, he was not given to projection. Meanwhile, he sought to forestall any possible suspicions his mother might come to entertain first by removing cheques from the back of her book and later by taking away the book altogether and letting her suppose it had been mislaid in the removal to Buckingham Terrace. It was hardly a brilliant manoeuvre, but it was, in the short run, surprisingly effective. Months later one of these cheque books was discovered in the boiler room of the Palais de Danse. The little matter of forgery came simply to him too. He merely traced his mother's signature in light pencil and then carefully inked it in. No doubt it was not a device to deceive an expert, but he had only bank clerks to deal with, and they were unlikely to suspect a university sudent, the only son of a respectable widow, domicilied in Buckingham Terrace, of so gross an offence as forgery. They had seen mother and son together, and had been impressed by their evident devotion to each other.

Clearly Donald was happy and insouciant, living in and for the moment, shinning down the tree out of his bedroom window and courting, or larking with, Miss Christie. If the thought of consequences ever touched his mind, he dismissed it; there was no place in his vocabulary for Nemesis. He had more immediate concerns and they were sufficient. However he was soon overtaken by events. A couple of days after they moved into the flat, the landlord called on Mrs Merrett. He asked her if she could now pay the balance of her rent, though this was not in fact due till later in the tenancy. However, being of an obliging nature, and conscious of the security of her financial state, she readily assented; she was by temperament one of those who prefer to be forward in payments due. Donald however remained ignorant of this transaction, which put his calculations out, for by chance Mrs Merrett paid the landlord with a Clydesdale cheque.

This cheque, being presented and honoured, overdrew the account. On Saturday 13 March therefore the bank wrote to Mrs Merrett, stating that her account was overdrawn by some £22, and requesting her to put things right. Donald apparently intercepted this letter, for Mrs Merrett did not then receive it. Instead on Tuesday 16th he corrected matters with a £30 Midland Bank cheque, payable to himself. He took £5 in cash. However he had already, the previous day, presented a Clydesdale cheque for £22.10.6. Accordingly on 16 March the Bank wrote again, pointing out that the account was now overdrawn by £6.11.3. This letter arrived on the morning of 17 March.

What happened that morning cannot be known in detail or certainty. Rita Sutherland, the maid, was the only witness, and she did not arrive till about nine o'clock. She discovered that Donald and his mother had already breakfasted. Mrs Merrett was putting the silver away. Then they settled in the sitting-room. If the subject of Donald's transgressions had

153

come up at the breakfast table, it seems that it had already been resolved. Certainly Rita Sutherland was not conscious of any argument or coolness between mother and son. She came into the drawing-room to do the fire, but finding Donald settled in the armchair with a book, and his mother preparing to write letters at the table which she used in preference to the desk, decided to do this later, and retired to the kitchen again. That was just across the narrow hall. Donald and his mother were sitting about eleven feet apart from each other.

A few minutes later Rita was startled by a loud bang. She heard quick-moving feet. Then a sound as of falling books, and Donald was in the kitchen. 'Rita', he cried, 'my mother has shot herself'. Either then, or a little later, she said that she had been quite all right when she herself arrived, and asked why she would do such a thing. He replied that, 'he had been wasting his mother's money and thought she was worried about that'. They found her lying on the floor, still breathing, between the table and the bureau. Rita 'noticed upon the top corner of the bureau, a pistol'. She had never seen it before.

Or perhaps she noticed it there. Any attempt to reconstruct exactly what happened and what she saw, is bedevilled by inconsistencies in her story — she was to tell two incompatible ones — and by the fact that, on certain points, notably the position of the pistol, her evidence conflicts with what others had to say.

Donald now telephoned for the police and told them that his mother had shot herself. His tone carried authority, so that this interpretation was to pass unquestioned for a long time. Then, finding the sight of his mother (who was still not dead) distressing, he suggested to Rita that they should go down to the street and wait for the ambulance that would take his mother to the hospital.

The police arrived first, in the form of two constables, Middlemiss and Izatt, decent deferential men, suitably chastened by the tragedy they encountered. Their attitude was to be of the first importance. They arrived less as 'investigators' than as 'the men come about the trouble'. Roughead, in his account of the trial, was to pour scorn upon them, suggesting that they might have been competent for a part in the Policemen's

Chorus in *The Pirates of Penzance*, But to elaborate on this – to dwell for instance on their inability to decide on the position of the pistol (one of them could not say, while the other stated that he saw his colleague lift it from the floor) – is to risk missing the point. No doubt they should have been brisk and inquisitive. That was not how they saw their job, not in a respectable place like Buckingham Terrace. Their attitude was quite different. Something very unfortunate had happened and they had better tidy it up. What else could have been expected of them, in a sitting-room where they would have considered it a solecism to take a chair? So they contented themselves with asking Donald, politely and modestly, if he had any idea why his mother should have shot herself. They nodded their heads at his airy reply – 'just money matters'. He could hardly have said anything more immediately convincing: everyone knew that money was serious business.

Mrs Merrett was taken off to the infirmary where she was confined in Ward 3, a security ward with barred windows, as a suspected suicide. Donald followed her there and inquired about her condition. 'Oh', he said, 'so it's still on the cards that she will recover?' He told the nurse that his mother had no friends in Edinburgh, which was of course a lie, and, as for her sisters, there was no use calling them, as 'they didn't get on'. One sister, Mrs Penn, was to deny this firmly; all the same Donald's counsel, Mr Aitchison, cast some doubt on what she said. Now, however, having done what he could to ensure that his mother would remain isolated in hospital, he betook himself to the Palais de Danse and Miss Christie. Popping her on the pillion of his motorbike, he went for a spin to Queensferry. Later in the afternoon they met their friend Scott. He told them what had happened and said Rita had been in the kitchen at the time of the shot.

All Donald's words and actions display inconsistency. One can only assume that he spoke and acted merely on whim. For very soon, he was sending a telegram to a friend of his mother called Mrs Hill, to summon her from Brighton. Even his callousness to his mother was not maintained. He was seen to kiss her on one of his visits; 'was it the kiss of Judas?' asked the Lord Justice-Clerk.

DONALD MERRETT

Similar inconsistency was to be shown by Rita Sutherland. That evening she was interviewed by Detective-Inspector Fleming, who had taken over the case. The story she told him was quite different. She now said 'she had been in the kitchen about 9.30 and heard a shot, and, going into the lobby, she saw Mrs Merrett fall off her chair and on to the floor and a pistol falling out of her hand.' Donald himself told Fleming that, 'he went over to the corner of the room and the next he heard was a shot, and that he looked round and saw his mother falling to the ground, with a revolver falling from her hand.' These two pieces of evidence corroborated each other. With the evident respectability of the setting, they were enough for Fleming. He had no doubts. Mrs Merrett had shot herself and he had two eye witnesses to prove it. Accordingly Sergeant Ross wrote to the hospital authorities asking that they should let the police know when Mrs Merrett was fit to leave hospital, that she might be taken into custody and charged with attempted suicide.

The wretched woman had meanwhile come round in Ward 3 to find herself almost in prison already. Barred windows, a locked door and an atmosphere of mystery and obfuscation oppressed her. Nobody would tell her what had happened, and she could not remember. There had been a little accident, they said, and would go no further. She said at different times, 'I was sitting writing at the table when suddenly a bang went off in my head like a pistol. . . .' and 'I was sitting down writing letters, and my son Donald was standing beside me. I said, "Go away, Donald, and don't annoy me", and the next I heard was a kind of explosion, and I don't remember any more.' Dr Holcombe of the Infirmary passed this report on to Inspect Fléming; he however, already certain of the facts, secure in his possession of eye witnesses' accounts, was not sufficiently impressed to interview her himself. As a result no deposition was ever taken from her.

Mrs Hill arrived and found her friend's condition distressing and puzzling. She could not believe in the suicide theory. She was to say that Mrs Merrett 'was highly strung, emotional, with a keen grip on life and everything it contained, but never a suggestion of doing away with herself.'. That was in no sense a conclusive judgement, and it was also one which offered hitherto unmentioned aspects of Mrs Merrett's character, but it was enough to convince Mrs Hill that something was wrong. Since she herself could not remain in Edinburgh, she summoned one of Mrs Merrett's sisters, a Mrs Penn. She duly arrived with her husband, a deaf and irascible painter, on 24 March, a week after the shooting. By her account, her sister repeated the same story of her last memory, and described the bang as seeming, 'as if Donald had shot me'. She then sought reassurance that he had not, and added, 'he is such a naughty boy'. Mrs Penn then aked Donald what had happened. Could he explain matters? His reply was flippant in the extreme: 'No, auntie, I did not do it, but if you like I will confess.' That raised an alarming interpretation of the affair that Mrs Penn was not at the time ready to accept. 'Nobody wants you to do that', she replied, and remained puzzled.

Such was the gist of Mrs Penn's evidence. If true, it certainly indicated that Mrs Merrett must have been tortured by the most horrible suspicion. But Mrs Penn was not an entirely disinterested witness. It was natural enough that she should have developed some animus against Donald. Moreover, Mr Aitchison elicited from her the interesting fact that, while Donald was the heir to his grandfather's property, her own son stood next in succession. He suggested to her that she herself had in fact asked Mrs Merrett whether Donald had shot her. She denied this vehemently, but since he was able to show that both she and her husband had been most reluctant to co-operate with the Defence, her denial was not wholly convincing.

Donald himself had not allowed his mother's condition to affect his way of life, except that he had for the moment moved out of the flat and taken a room in a hotel in Lothian Road; all his life he was to delight in hotel life; it satisfied his immature craving for make-believe. Otherwise he had continued on his merry way. The cheque book was now freely available, and, while his mother lived, he made the most of it, drawing £156 in the nine days he had the use of it. This included the down payment on an HRD racing motorbike, valued at £139. He could of course have bought it outright

157

DONALD MERRETT

with one Midland Bank cheque, but that was not his way. Credit was to his taste; the day of reckoning might be as far removed or even mythical as God's judgement. On the bike, or in company with Mis Christie or his friend Scott, he had a few jolly days. Calling at the hospital on one occasion, he was pressed by the nurse to give her a telephone number where he could be reached should his mother's condition deteriorate. He asked her to wait a moment, while he stepped into the waiting-room to consult Miss Christie. He returned with a number which was in fact that of the Dunedin.

At last on 27 March Mrs Merrett died. The immediate cause of death was basal meningitis. She had never learned why she was in the hospital. She must have passed many painful and distressing hours wondering what had happened, for certainly she had no recollection of having herself fired a shot or accidentally dislodged the pistol. She can hardly have failed to suffer from the horrid fear which Mrs Penn ascribed to her, whether she in fact uttered it or not, for her last memory was of Donald standing over her, while she wrote a letter to her friend, Miss Anderson. And then the bang. (Donald said she had put the wrong address on the envelope, which he was waiting to take to the Post.)

Her death brought his madcap career to a temporary halt. Even Donald could see that he could not continue to forge the cheques of a dead woman. His uncle and aunt temporarily took him in hand. In theory he continued his studies at the university, while they all took up residence together at Buckingham Terrace. It seemed as if the affair slept. Mrs Penn still probed and questioned, but the police had accepted the case as one of suicide. That was that. Donald, perhaps in response to his aunt's questioning, perhaps simply for a lark, set off to London with Miss Christie and Scott ostensibly to consult a famous detective. Predictably they returned without one, their money exhausted, having had to hitch a lift on a lorry. Coldness prevailed in Buckingham Terrace. The summer wore on. The university indicated a preference for Donald's absence the next year. What was to be done with the boy?

Fortunately, that was not the Penns' problem. Mrs Merrett's will had entrusted the management of her estate and the guardianship of her son to the Public Trustee, an action which has attracted curiously little attention. Yet surely it was unusual enough? Mrs Merrett had family, two sisters at least. It might have been thought that these would prove more suitable guardians than a necessarily remote civil servant. Her choice suggests therefore either that her relations with her sisters had hitherto been bad, just as Donald said they were, or that she had some secret reason. This could only have been a distrust of Donald. On the face of it simply a doting mother, Mrs Merrett yet showed by her actions in several respects that she had, doubtless reluctantly, come to understand that Donald, though possibly brilliant, might not be altogether normal; that he was certainly not absolutely reliable. The Malvern experience had opened her eyes. Her decision to come to Edinburgh and the comparatively small allowance she gave Donald were evidence. It may be that she had for some time now realised that Donald might need careful attention. Hence the Public Trustee. In short Mrs Merrett may not have been altogether a fool with regard to her son.

The Public Trustee soon had his doubts also. In the summer, preparatory to a decision as to the boy's future, he had him medically examined. The report was reassuring, up to a point. 'The lad is exceptionally developed physically for his age (in later life Merrett was to weigh twenty-two stone) and looks at least over twenty years. He talks intelligently and confidently, and is clear and lucid in his statements on general topics . . . mentally he is perfectly sane. . . .' The last observation suggests that doubts had arisen. It is possible that these had been shared by Mrs Merrett; and what of his emotional condition? Still the examination was sufficiently reassuring for the Public Trustee to decide to revive the old Oxford plan. Donald was therefore sent south to prepare for entry.

Circumstances, the march of events, over which Donald had by his own actions abandoned any control, so that, thinking himself free, he was actually caught in a web of his own spinning, forestalled the proposal. Investigation of Mrs Merrett's finances, necessary for Probate, revealed the irregularities of the spring months, sufficiently at variance with her normal practice to give birth to doubts. What had been happening? Why should so careful and prudent a woman have embarked on a course of unprecedented extravagance? And then there were the dates on the cheques, suggesting that Mrs Merrett had run through a hundred and fifty odd pounds – to say nothing of buying a motorbike – while she lay virtually a prisoner, fighting for her life in Ward 3 of Edinburgh Royal Infirmary. It would not do; obviously there was something fishy, and obviously, Donald, to whom most of the cheques were payable, was the villain. The police interest revived. Evidence of Donald's forgery put a new complexion on his mother's death. Here was motive. A warrant was issued on 29 November, executed by the local police a few days later, and Donald was committed on 9 December charged with murder and forgery. He was indicted on 14 January, and the trial began on 1 February almost a year after his mother's death.

The case for the Prosecution, conducted by the Lord Advocate, depended first on the evidence of Donald's financial misdemeanours, then on the evidence offered by Rita Sutherland. Mrs Merrett's state of mind was also germane, for it was necessary to pre-empt a Defence line which would adhere to the original police theory of suicide; embarrassing in the circumstances. Beyond that, it was deemed necessary for the Crown to show that the circumstances of the shooting were inconsistent with either suicide or accident. If the nature of the wound ruled these out, then it followed that Mrs Merrett had been shot by someone else, and there could be no candidate but Donald, who was admittedly and incontestably alone in the room with his mother when the shot was heard. If, on the other hand, the Crown failed to establish these points, if Rita's evidence could be shaken, or the Crown's expert witnesses proved unconvincing, then it was clear that the Crown would have failed to produce arguments sufficiently powerful to outweigh the prejudice caused by the long delay in bringing the case, and the natural repugnance on the part of any jury to convict a personable young man of such an unnatural crime. There could be little doubt that the clumsy and impercipient police handling of the case had made conviction very much more difficult.

On the first point, Donald's financial transactions, there

was little problem in making the case. Certainly the bank clerks who had cashed the cheques still obstinately refused to see anything wrong with them, but the authority of the hand-writing expert was hard to contest. Moreover, even if Donald had been a forger of the most exquisite skill nothing could have explained away the £156 obtained while his mother lay confined and powerless in the infirmary. The Defence put forward the argument that Mrs Merrett could have signed cheques with some assistance – but they did not push it hard. Wisely enough, for common sense would have been offended at the notion that the dying woman should have written cheques for motor-bicycles. That granted, any suggestion that Donald had perhaps commenced forgery only after the shooting was too ludicrous to advance. On the fact of forgery the Defence barely existed. Whether Mrs Merrett discovered it and whether such discovery afforded sufficient motive were however other matters, and more debatable ones.

Rita Sutherland's evidence was a good deal less satisfactory, for it could not be denied that she had told two separate and conflicting stories. The first of these, that she had been in the kitchen at the time of the shot, left the issue open. The second that she had actually 'seen Mrs Merrett fall off the chair and on to the floor and a pistol falling out of her hand' would of course have acquitted Donald. It was this story which had fixed the idea of suicide in Inspector Fleming's mind. The fact that she now denied this second story absolutely and had returned to her first could not wholly eradicate the impression that it made. A jury is always in difficulties with a witness who has changed his story. Inconsistency equals unreliability at the least. One story, being untrue, may be a deliberate lie. When do you believe a liar? If not a lie, it is evidence of confusion. How can one determine just where the witness is confused and where he or she is clear? It is a question to which there is rarely a certain answer. Either Rita's original statement to which she had now returned, was false, or the one she had offered to Inspector Fleming was a lie. The Defence was able to produce a witness, a certain Dr Rosa, who was ready to swear that Rita had come to him, with the eye witness story also, on the evening of the shooting. He added that she had said that she had seen Mrs Merrett remove her false teeth just before the shot. That was a remarkable detail, even if not one that was necessarily convincing. Rita now dismissed Dr Rosa's story as 'a downright lie', and it is easy enough to invent a motive for his coming forward. All the same her change of story is hard to explain. She herself said she was confused when she spoke to Fleming; she never said what had happened to confuse her between the morning and evening of 17 March. Perhaps she told the eye witness story merely to make herself seem more important, and then retracted it when she saw where it was leading. Had her original version not been reinforced by what Donald said that same day to Miss Christie and Scott, her credibility as a witness would have been slight indeed.

It was even harder to determine Mrs Merrett's state of mind. The Crown had to show that she was not suicidal. Character evidence was uniformly favourable, though Mrs Hill's assertion that Mrs Merrett was 'highly strung, emotional', was open to an interpretation that differed from hers. Mr Aitchison asked Mrs Penn whether there was no madness in the family. That was not a line likely to be very potent; for one thing it might equally well lead to Donald. Mrs Penn's reply was firm enough; there was a case of madness, but it was not of a hereditary sort. In any case there was no evidence that could have led anyone to question Mrs Merrett's sanity, apart from the shooting itself. The fact that she had been engaged in writing a letter to an old friend at the moment the shot was heard was surely powerful evidence that she had not killed herself wilfully. Moreover the contents of the letter were hardly a preliminary to sucide. She told her old friend, Mrs Anderson, that she had at last found a flat and a maid; then presumably, bang. It is, to say the least, unusual for someone to break off such a letter in order to put a pistol to the temple. Curiously, the letter disappeared. Donald told the police that he had thrown it away because it was bloodstained; the police constables had seen no such stains, but the jury could not be blamed if they had come to the conclusion that Izatt and Middlemiss could have waded ankle deep in blood without noticing its presence. The inference to be drawn from

Donald's act was that he realised that the letter was hardly that of a suicide and so decided it should disappear. There was though something else odd about the letter which seems to have escaped comment. The theory of murder rests on the presumption that the Bank's letter had caused Mrs Merrett to question Donald and that this questioning had disclosed his guilty secret. All this must have happened in quite a short time, for Rita Sutherland heard no quarrel or angry words. Instead she saw Donald settling down to read a book, and his mother to write letters; a calm domestic scene; but hardly perhaps a satisfactory prelude to murder. It is possible, that the matter had not yet been broached; that would mean that Donald shot his mother to forestall any inquiry. What happened between them rests entirely on Donald's statement that, 'he had been wasting his mother's money and thought she was worried about that.' But it is hard to base credence on anything he said.

What was recorded of Mrs Merrett's conversation in the infirmary all tended to confirm the Crown's case. She had been sitting writing letters, Donald had come and stood over her in a manner she found irritating. She had asked him to move away and then heard a bang in her head. It all pointed to a conclusion that she was naturally disinclined to draw; there could be no reason however for the jury to share her reluctance. To her question 'Donald didn't do it, did he? He is such a naughty boy' they were likely to return an answer untainted by affection. It was necessary therefore for the Defence to try to discredit her memory, even though the Lord Justice-Clerk was to point out in his charge to the jury that no one at the time had thought her various observations made in the infirmary involved Donald's guilt. The murder charge had been 'an after-thought'.

Still the Defence could not rely on that. They called as an expert witness Dr George Robertson, Professor of Mental Diseases at the University of Edinburgh and Head of the Morningside Lunatic Asylum. Like many fellow-maestri Dr Robertson had come almost to believe that insanity was everywhere to be found. Roughead remarked, in a memorable phrase, that 'his mastery of his art was such that he could have proved Solomon senile and Solon certifiable.' Now he put forward the notion that Mrs Merrett might have been suffering, while in hospital, from what he termed 'altered consciousness', 'Dissociation might be the correct term to use.' Its effect might easily be to impair the memory. So Mrs Merrett would remember things clearly up to a few minutes before the accident and then experience an absolute obliteration of memory. She could easily in consequence omit incidents, telescope time or something of that sort. It was 'quite possible that the interval of time that elapsed between when Mrs Merrett found her son beside her and the explosion took place was very much longer than is suspected'. Nothing could be more convenient than that for the Defence. Memory in such cases was frequently distorted also; Professor Robertson was happy to give instances . . . furthermore the fact that neither doctors nor nurses in the infirmary had noticed anything wrong with Mrs Merrett, could not, as far as Professor Robertson was concerned, be allowed to cut very much ice. Far from it: 'these people', said he, in a phrase reeking of the self-conscious superiority of the expert, 'these people pay very little attention to mental symptoms. That is pointed out in the Report of the Royal Commission . . . how defective the training is in this subject.' If you believed Professor Robertson then – and who could entirely discount such sublime assurance? – then no matter how lucid and sensible Mrs Merrett had seemed to nursing staff and physicians, to her sister and other visitors, no credence could be given to anything she had said in her condition. She might of course be quite correct – Professor Robertson was too wily a bird to rule out that possibility completely – but, suffering from 'altered consciousness', she could be quite, quite wrong. After this performance Mr Aitchison could confidently bid the jury ignore the evidence of what she had said, what she had remembered (evidence which he had tried and failed to have excluded) except where it was independently confirmed.

If you believed Professor Robertson . . . that was the problem, for the learned Professor was only one expert in a case as crammed with sages as a tin with sardines. The whole question of the pistol, the distance from which it had been fired, and the nature of the wound, as well as Mrs Merrett's mental condition, was in the hand of experts. The courtroom became like the lists of a medieval tournament, as heavily armoured expert clashed mightily with counter-expert.

First, for the Crown, was Professor Harvey Littlejohn, Police Surgeon, the latest in that remarkable dynasty. He was supported byDr Bell and by Professor Glaister of Glasgow University, and he needed that support. For Littlejohn was in an awkward spot. Like Rita Sutherland he had changed his mind and his story with it, and this invariably induces discomfort in an expert; far easier for mere housemaids to accommodate such contradiction. Littlejohn had made the original post-mortem examination. At that time he had felt, and, worse, stated, that, 'there was nothing to indicate the distance at which the discharge took place, whether from a few inches or a greater distance'. Accordingly there was nothing in the nature of the wound incompatible with suicide. That was lucidity indeed, and at the time perfectly satisfactory, since it agreed with the police interpretation of the case. Now however things had changed. The Crown had determined to prosecute. Professor Littlejohn was a Crown witness and suicide had become out of the question. Had it been a case of suicide, they would have found evidence of blackening around the wound, but there was none. The absence of blackening, immaterial a few months before, had now taken on vast significance; Professor Glaister agreed that blackening was a *sine qua non* of suicide. Clearly therefore the discharge had been at a distance greater than a few inches. It was perhaps a pity that Professor Littlejohn had not at once come to this conclusion; still he had got there now, and found himself reinforced by the other experts.

Then there was the position of the wound. At one time he had said, 'so far as the position of the wound is concerned the case is consistent with suicide'. Now he found that, 'the hand and arm would be in a strained position'. 'All in all therefore I am of the opinion that suicide was in the highest degree improbable. The direction of the bullet, the position of the wound, and the distance at which the discharge took place, all point to the weapon having been fired by a third party. To my

DONALD MERRETT

mind suicide is is inconceivable from the facts I know. Yet the same facts had existed at the time of the post-mortem; no new medical evidence had been produced. It was all a matter of interpretation and judgement. Mr Aitchison pursued him hard: 'if the evidence of Dr Holcombe be right that he had to cleanse the wound thoroughly, can you be certain that it would not remove blackening or tattooing if they were there?' He had driven him to the point of admitting that the theory he now put forward depended on the distance of the discharge; if that were displaced then neither suicide not accident could be discounted. (In fact accident did not depend on the question of the distance.) Professor Littlejohn was forced to yield ground, but still proclaimed that, even so, suicide had become inconceivable to him. It was dogged at least; he had changed his mind once, he was not going to do so again. He showed the same obstinacy with regard to Mrs Merrett's mental condition: 'If a person shows no signs of abnormality and then becomes wandered in the mind, surely up to the time that she shows signs of wandering she is normal.' It might not be much to set against theories of altered consciousness, but it showed common sense at least. All Mr Aitchison could do was throw up his hands and exclaim, 'If experts differ, what are we to do in the matter? I don't know.' And that was fair enough too, besides being good theatre.

The Defence experts were mostly imported from the South. The famous London gunsmith, Robert Churchill, was the first of these. The Crown had already produced an Edinburgh gunsmith, one Macnaghten, who had ridiculed the pistol itself. This had been bought by Donald – there was no doubt about, no denial of, that – though his reasons for the purchase varied. In one version it had been bought for shooting rabbits on the Braid Hills, in another because he was going on holiday in France, as if everyone knew that a weapon was necessary if you intended to make so dangerous a tour. (Perhaps he had been reading too much Dornford Yates.) In Macnaghten's view the pistol was quite useless for shooting rabbits, far too short in the barrel; only of some use for self-defence. Such strictures were actually irrelevant. They proved nothing beyond the fact that Donald was a rotten judge of

166

firearms and had no idea what to buy; that he had been ill-advised by the shop where he bought it. Nobody had suggested that the murder was premeditated, that he had bought the pistol with the intention of shooting his mother. And if he had, it was still a poor choice, since Mrs Merrett had lingered ten days after the shooting, mothers being at least as hard to kill as rabbits.

All that was rather pointless, Churchill's evidence for the Defence being a good deal more formidable. He dealt arrogantly enough with the Crown case. His whole pose, well justified of course, was that of the man of infinite experience. He had no difficulty in believing in the possibility of either suicide or accident. He could explain anything away. Take the absence of blackening for example. He, Churchill, taught shooting and he had found that women generally flinched when firing weapons. It was 'an instinctive aversion'. The result might easily be to jerk the head away so that the bullet might, even in a case of suicide, be fired quite far from the head. It was unfortunate of course that this premonitory jerk had not taken the wretched Mrs Merrett's head altogether out of the line of fire; but, though this point wasn't made, the fact that death had not been instantaneous, that the shot had been in a sense botched, might be held to support Churchill's argument. What was more, there were all sorts of conceivable ways in which her death could have been the result of an accident. The fact that the trigger required a pull of five pounds was not conclusive. She could easily have knocked the pistol off the bureau, with fatal consequences. Accidents were extremely various. Then again, the position of the wound proved nothing, even apart from the premonitory jerk. Churchill had known of a case where a woman had shot herself behind the ear. Finally, asked whether he had ever heard of a woman shooting herself in the presence of a near relative, he was up to that improbability too. Yes, he had known of a woman who had shot herself sitting in an armchair by the fireside while her husband slept in his chair on the other side of the hearth. In short Churchill's evidence offered a masterly exhibition of scepticism.

He was followed by the most celebrated and impressive of

the Defence witnesses, no less a person, even a personage, than Sir Bernard Spilsbury, famed in the popular press and known to every *aficionado* of murder as the Home Office pathologist. Spilsbury was indeed the *crème de la crème*, the expert of experts. Normally of course he appeared for the Crown, being retained by the Home Office. His appearance in this unfamiliar role, possible only because the trial was taking place in Scotland, added new drama and piquancy. Securing his services had been an undoubted coup. Spilsbury, who always gave the impression of not thinking too badly of himself, clearly relished his new part. Courtrooms were his theatre. Now he set to work to demolish the Crown's theories. Like Churchill his line was one of an infinitely experienced and wordly scepticism. Yes, indeed, one would normally expect blackening around a wound when a pistol had been held close to the head. Dr Bell, 'who had looked for any sign of blackening but found none', was certainly correct, as far as he went. Only, said Spilsbury, 'the bleeding from and rubbing of the wound might have removed blackening'. Morever, he had tested a pistol of the same calibre against cardboard from contact to a distance of six inches away and found very little blackening. Pistols differed in their effect. Then, when he had repeated the test against pieces of skin, the blackening had been still less distinct than on cardboard and had been more easily washed away. It was impossible to rely on blackening.

The nature of the wound was equally inconclusive. In the first place, 'almost any suicidal wound may be imitated by a homicidal wound'. Then, and he demonstrated this, it was perfectly possible for someone to shoot themselves when holding the pistol in a quite extraordinary position. He himself could recall the case of a man who had shot himself from half an inch behind his right ear, and the bullet passed out immediately above the left ear. That showed what could happen. Moreover, 'it would be easy for a woman, who would have considerable shoulder joint movement owing to her doing up her hair' to shoot herself from an unusual angle. Accident could not be ruled out either. 'In my own experience' he said, 'most extraordinary positions sometimes result from the accidental discharge'. Who could ignore such authority?

Finally, turning to what Mrs Merrett had said, or was reported to have said, in hospital, he aligned himself firmly with Professor Robertson. 'I think that any such statements must be accepted with great caution', he said. 'May such statement', Mr Aitchison asked, 'appear to be made by a person of normal mentality, whose mentality is in fact abnormal'. Sir Bernard's reply was simple and certain: 'Yes.' The effect of his scepticism was great. There was no reason to exclude anything. He, Spilsbury, with the authority of a lifetime, found 'nothing inconsistent with suicide or accident'.

As in the Chantrelle case the conflicting testimony of the experts made things difficult for the jury. That must almost always be the case; indeed it may be questioned how much of such expert evidence a jury ever really follows. To put this point of view is not to denigrate the intelligence of jurymen. The fact is that evidence of this sort is usually hard enough to grasp even in printed form. Reading the accounts of trials, one has constantly to retrace one's steps in an attempt to understand exactly what experts are saying. Jurymen probably rely on the trained intelligence of the Judge to make things clear to them, to cut a swathe through the web of words, or guide them through the labyrinth of technical language. But when one expert contradicts another, even Judges may be in difficulty.

In the end it may be that a good deal of expert evidence merely wastes time, the jury being impressed more by character as they perceive it than by argument. If this is so, and both common sense and experience suggest it is, much of the argument really turns not on what is possible, but on what seems probable. Yet possibilities are often discussed at greater length in Court. That certainly happened in the Merrett case. Hours were spent arguing about the distance of the discharge and the position of the wound. Yet clearly enough inconsistencies of experience abound in such matters. The most extraordinary accidents do occur; one does not have to be a writer of detective stories of the ingenuity of a Michael Innes or Dorothy L. Sayers to see that. It is not of course surprising that time should be consumed in this sort of argument, since those experts deal in what is apparently susceptible of scientific verification. Nevertheless, in the last resort, this case did not really turn on the presence or absence of blackening, whatever Mr Aitchison may have persuaded a reluctant Littlejohn to admit. Certainly if there was blackening, suicide, accident and murder were all possible, though the chances of suicide were somewhat improved. Equally certainly, the absence of blackening did not absolutely exclude suicide, though it made the chances of murder rather greater. But that was all there was to it. The technical evidence, offered by so glittering an array of experts, settled precisely nothing. (It may of course be objected that the technical evidence could have persuaded them one way or another, and that different technical evidence might have been decisive; that all I am saying is that here the technical evidence was too contradictory to be conclusive. But that is frequently the case; experts can always be recruited and their evidence is sometimes specious and rarely unimpeachable.)

It came down therefore to a question of what the jury believed about Donald and Mrs Merrett. Did they believe that Mrs Merrett, sitting writing that letter to an old friend, in which she told her that she had at last acquired a satisfactory flat and a maid, should suddenly, in the presence of her only child, whip out a pistol, plant it against her head and pull the trigger? And what was the motive assigned? She was distressed and shocked that Donald, whose behaviour hitherto had not always been exemplary, but to whom she was devoted, should have been discovered to be a forger and utterly unreliable. A painful shock certainly, but sufficient to persuade the jury that it was cause to blow her brains out? They could hardly accept that proposition without abandoning the conviction that Mrs Merrett was a reasonable and sane person. It was hardly the act of 'a cheerful and bright woman, a person of methodical habits, never seen in an excitable state'. Nothing that was learned of Mrs Merrett at the trial made suicide seem likely, whatever Sir Bernard Spilsbury might say was possible. Certainly not this sort of suicide; one could imagine her taking an overdose, but not blowing her brains out before her beloved son.

What of Donald and the case for murder? Nobody on the

jury can have thought Donald anything other than a rather odd fish. The boisterous immaturity of his behaviour, his silly-clever duplicity, his callousness, all were evidence of a disturbed and thoroughly unreliable personality. He looked an odd fish too. A photograph taken of him as he arrived at the Court shows him peering out from under a huge brimmed felt hat, through horn-rimmed Harold Lloyd spectacles. The mouth is curiously long and flat, the mouth of a predatory fish, a pike for instance. A loose collar, with no tie, stands away from the neck. Nor was his behaviour any more pre-possessing. The *Evening Dispatch* reporter said that he showed 'a smiling unconcern' on the first day of the trial, even as his lies were uncovered. And he had lied with a frequency and ease that spoke of long practice, and a total disregard for truth, amounting even to an inability to recognise it. He had lied about his reasons for buying the pistol. More seriously he had lied about his mother's knowledge of the pistol, for he had first said she did not know he had it, then that she not only knew but had taken it away from him. This time the reason for the change of story was obvious: Mrs Merrett could hardly have killed herself with a pistol which she did not know to exist.

All the same the lies, oddity and general unreliability did not quite amount to a convincing proof of murder. Some-thing more was needed; what was offered was unsatisfactory. Motive is always a problem. The Lord Justice-Clerk had weighty and wise advice to offer the jury on the subject. Proof of a motive to commit a crime, however important, would not do in the absence of sufficient evidence to prove the com-mission of a crime. Even if they were satisfied that a crime had been committed and that there was a motive, they must still ask themselves whether the motive suggested was at all commensurate with the crime suggested. And that undoubt-edly offered a difficulty. Donald had, one assumes, been found out, or was at least on the point of being discovered. But nothing very dreadful was likely to happen to him. There would be a row, may even have been one before Rita arrived, but it would blow over, amount to nothing more than a spot of unpleasantness. Nobody could doubt that Mrs Merrett

DONALD MERRETT

would soon have forgiven Donald. Nobody could doubt that he would not have been able to extricate himself with a show of penance. Could it really be believed that he would kill merely to escape a spot of unpleasantness? Was he that abnormal?

Common sense tends to begin with the question of motive whatever Judges may sagely advise. But here, even if the motive could be swallowed, the question of the mechanics of the crime remained uncertain. Rita Sutherland saw mother and son in their sittingroom, mother writing letters, son in the armchair reading a book. She then went through to the kitchen. In a few minutes Donald gets up, puts down his book, stands over his mother, ready to take her letter to the post. Then when she says, 'Go away, Donald, you are bothering me' – a phrase which suggests a pretty low emotional temperature and one that both confirm – he takes out his pistol and shoots her; then picks up his books, drops them on the floor, goes through to the kitchen and says 'Rita, my mother has shot herself . . .' The jury could be forgiven for thinking that that made little sense either. Furthermore, as the Lord Justice-Clerk pointed out, 'the gunshot was fired in the flat at the time when Mrs Sutherland was there. It might have been fired quite easily in her absence.' Why wait till she was there? She might have come into the room at the wrong moment. A witness on the spot is hardly what the prudent murderer desires.

What of accident? The experts had shown that it was physically possible. Yet three points might be made against this interpretation of events. First, it was simply too well timed, too apt that Mrs Merrett should have a fatal accident just when Donald's malfeasances had come to light; it was all too pat. Second, though physically possible, it was inherently unlikely in the absence of any supporting evidence. Third, which may be held to be the most powerful argument against the accident theory, were Donald's words – 'Rita, my mother has shot herself . . .' That fixed his interpretation or the one he was putting forward. Otherwise the natural thing to say would have been, 'there's been an accident . . .'

The jury's dilemma was that none of the explanations made

sense. They all involved improbabilities that reason rejected. Least objectionable was murder; all that required was to believe that Donald Merrett was abnormal, though certainly not in any legal sense mad, that he had no moral scruples and an unusually demanding ego. Even so, a douce rate-paying church-going Edinburgh jury was going to find it hard to believe that a wellborn youth from the respectable classes could possibly commit so ghastly a murder for such frivolous reasons.

Probably the long delay before Donald's arrest told in his favour, though his Counsel proclaimed otherwise. The fact that suicide had been accepted unquestioningly at the time, and that nobody, as the Lord Justice-Clerk remarked, had then understood Mrs Merrett's words in the infirmary as involving her son's guilt, made the trial appear a sort of afterthought, consequent to and dependent on, the charge of forgery. The police's working assumption had been suicide. Certainly this meant that investigation at the time had been lax, that the question of Mrs Merrett's knowledge of the pistol had not been thoroughly examined and that the conflict of Rita Sutherland's two stories had been ignored. Moreover, the long delay meant that witnesses' memories were more than usually unreliable and the failure to take a dying deposition from Mrs Merrett had even allowed the Defence to call in question the admissibility of evidence relating to her version of events. There were simply too many contradictions and unexplained revisons of evidence for any jury to feel confident. When Mr Aitchison said that, 'he could not understand how the Lord Advocate could throw over the evidence of Inspector Fleming and Dr Rosa and ask them to accept the revised version of Mrs Sutherland . . .', the conscientious juryman could only nod his head in sympathetic agreement. After all, he might have thought, what Rita Sutherland said to the Inspector and to Dr Rosa was absolutely clear and established the certainty of suicide . . . I may myself prefer her revised version, but can I be absolutely sure. . . .? And that is what I need . . . certainty. . . .

Mr Aitchison made a frank appeal to sentiment. Roughead was to describe his closing address as one of the two best he ever heard; and yet it contained hardly any real argument. It was directed at the emotions, not at the intellect; and in this Mr Aitchison was almost certainly wise. For it was clear enough that the case logically tended towards an admission of murder, however improbable it might seem, if only because all other explanations seemed still less likely; eliminate the impossible, and whatever remains, however improbable, must be the truth. Yet proof was not clinching; it could be upset by sentiment. He laid it on thick. 'I say with the utmost respect that if you send this lad into life with the verdict of Not Proven, with the stigma which it implies upon him, you are taking a tremendous responsibility on your shoulders. . . .' That was clever. It implied that they could not convict but admitted that they were unlikely to acquit. The word 'lad', not very apt when one looks at photographs of Merrett, with his hooded heavy predatory features, emphasized the Jury's responsibility; it was almost as if they were *in loco parentis* to the orphaned Donald; they were the men who would decide his future. Concerning that though Mr Aitchison was ready with promises too: 'Send out this lad a free man with a clean bill and, so far as I can judge, he will never dishonour your verdict'. That was asking a bit much, asking them indeed to conflate the murder charge where the evidence was certainly dubious and unsatisfactory with the forgery one where doubt of Donald's guilt was hardly possible.

The jury found that part of their task easy. Their debate on the murder charge came to less than might have been expected. They were out for only fifty-five minutes. That suggests they took an essentially common sense view of the matter, that they quickly agreed that the technical question had not been resolved and that anything being possible, murder, suicide or accident, the matter just fell back on the simple question; 'Do you think he did it?' They took a vote: five said Guilty; ten thought it 'Not Proven'. For all Mr Aitchison's eloquence, nobody was prepared to say 'Not Guilty'.

Their verdict was fair enough. Sufficient doubt remained. Yet few, free of responsibility in the affair, have ever hesitated to proclaim Donald guilty. The chances are indeed strong that he did it. The term 'miscarriage of justice' is often restricted to cases where an innocent man is convicted; it may equally fairly be applied to a case like this one, where a guilty man goes free. One cannot help feeling that any thorough and efficient police investigation at the time would have resulted in a more convincing Crown case, offering fewer loopholes and a less easy access to sentiment.

He was sent down for twelve months on the forgery charge, a sentence he greeted 'with stoical calm'. A considerable crowd outside the High Court cheered him as he emerged, cigarette in mouth and dived into a van. That was rather strange; he might have been more fairly regarded as a monster. He was seen to wave in jaunty style to two friends, possibly Miss Christie and Scott, more probably the self-styled Lady Menzies, with whom he had been lodging at the time of his arrest, and her daughter whom he was to marry. He served his sentence in the new prison of Saughton. Roughead was properly indignant, describing it as 'a sort of penal garden-city, affording in its humane and hygienic regime the advantages of a rest-cure, a criminous nursing home, and combining agreeably punishment with amusement.' Some exaggeration there, and a view of Saughton more easily held from Belgrave Crescent, just behind Buckingham Terrace itself, where Roughead lived, assiduously and delightedly recording crime in bland ignorance of the stresses that may promote it. Still, in this case, the old man's scepticism was well enough founded. Not only did Donald Merrett emerge to a life of swindling, false pretences, smuggling, gun-running, black marketeering, all interspersed with spells in British and Continental jails, but eventually, in 1954, exasperated by his wife's refusal to give him a divorce, infatuated with a German blonde, and wanting to get his hands on money which he had made over to his wife, he tried to bring off a second 'perfect murder'; and botched it, had to kill his mother-in-law as well (clumsily); found that at last his luck had run out; and shot himself in a wood in Germany. So he capped a pointless life, dead to morality, concerned with nothing more than the gratification of the immediate instant. Deeply unpleasant, superficially charming, never advancing beyond the imperative of 'I want', there can be

DONALD MERRETT

little doubt that Donald Merrett was lucky that Edinburgh spring, little doubt either that he was saved by the prim and unimpeachable respectability of Buckingham Terrace.

Index

INDEX